Water from Heaven

To my parents, Marge and Tom,

and to Cindy's parents, Gladys and R.G.,

for having the wisdom to let us go.

"I had many dreams. I dreamt of our land
keeping pace with the growth of the modern world."

– Sheikh Zayed bin Sultan al Nahyan,
founder of the United Arab Emirates

Sheikh Zayed, center, discussing the mock-up
of UAE University in 1974
Source: UAE Archives

Water from Heaven

An American Woman's Life as an Arab Wife

Anne Schreiber Thomas

Table of Contents

Map of the United Arab Emirates

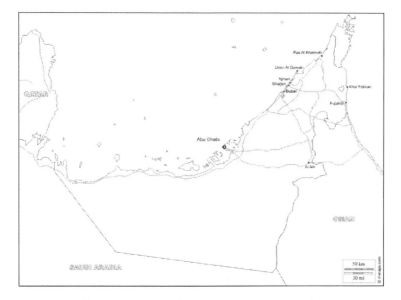

Source: http://www.d-maps.com/carte.php?num_car=50727&lang=en

Preface

Sometimes things happen in totally unexpected ways, and for reasons that are only revealed over time. This book is testament to that. In 2011, my husband Mark got an unexpected offer to work in Abu Dhabi, in the United Arab Emirates (UAE) – a place we knew almost nothing about. At the same time, the funding for my nonprofit job ran out, and I became unemployed. Within a few months, we were living in the Middle East, an adventure that lasted from September of 2011 through December of 2014.

Mark worked for an American company as a consultant to the Emirati military. He often came home with anecdotes about the people he worked with. Many were Emirati nationals who were a mixture of Arab culture and Western influence, having studied in the U.S. One day Mark told me about a guy at work, who was always saying funny things that made him sound like an American. His name was Mohammed Ali.

"His wife is American. They've been married for almost 30 years. She's from North Carolina. Mohammed invited us to visit them." This invitation to visit, coming from an Arab, was no idle chatter. If you are invited you must go, and be prepared to be treated like royalty. In just a couple of weeks we'd made our plans.

Mohammed and Cindy lived in Khorfakkan, a small town in the UAE's Eastern Region on the Gulf of Oman. We booked a hotel in Fujairah, about 30 minutes south of Khorfakkan. Before the weekend arrived, I emailed and called Cindy to introduce myself and check on their schedule for the weekend. Cindy asked if I had any kids.

"Two, grown up and living in California, and a granddaughter. And you?" I said.

"Three. Two girls in their 20's and a boy, 17. All still live at home." The Eastern Region was quite a contrast to both Abu Dhabi and

Dubai, Cindy told me. Life was slower paced and more relaxed. Her voice was quiet and calm, and I caught a southern twang. "It's nice here," she said.

Being a geographer, I did some research and learned that Fujairah and Khorfakkan were in a jigsaw puzzle of land controlled by the United Arab Emirates and the Sultanate of Oman. As the only cities on the Arabian Peninsula's eastern seaboard belonging to the UAE, they were important ports – the UAE's only access to the world's oceans without passing through the politically treacherous Strait of Hormuz. We took a scenic southern route over the Hajar Mountains and north along the coastline, a mix of shipping facilities interspersed with small towns, historic villages, and beaches. We saw beat-up Toyota pickups parked on the sand as the fishermen dragged their nets out in small open boats. Further on, enormous storage tanks.

That weekend, we spent the better part of two days with Mohammed and Cindy. The first day we visited *Al Bidyah*, the oldest mosque in the Emirates, and drove north to Dibba, a town divided into three sections and controlled by two countries but three governments – Oman and two Emirates of the UAE, Fujairah and Sharjah. We also saw the old abandoned village by the sea where Mohammed was born, we drove past several huge oceanside resorts under development, and then into the foothills to see the colorful, historic Omani doors and gates that are the region's architectural signature.

We had dinner with the family at a Lebanese restaurant on the Corniche road overlooking the Gulf of Oman, watching locals cruising the strip below us in an Arab version of American Graffiti. The next day we went to Mohammed and Cindy's for a home-cooked Arab meal before heading back over the mountains to Abu Dhabi.

That first weekend that Cindy and I met, she talked about how she came to live in the UAE. "People tell me I should write a book with all these stories I have," she said, "but I'm not a writer and besides, I don't really have the time."

"Hmm," I thought. An idea was hatching.

A couple of months later, Mark and I went back for a beach resort weekend on the coast. We were once again treated to lunch with

Mohammed, Cindy, and family, and I suggested to Cindy that I would like to write her story. In June, we attended their 30th wedding anniversary party, and I knew then that theirs was a story that must be told.

The next month, I went back to Khorfakkan by myself. For three days and two nights during the week of July 4th I stayed with Cindy, Aminah, Aisha, and Faisal. Mohammed was working and living on base, as he had throughout their married life – only coming home on weekends.

I was charmed by the family. Aminah, who worked as a teaching assistant, was quiet but once she started talking she went a mile a minute, telling stories in English about her students or bantering with her mother and siblings in Arabic. Although Aminah didn't have a teaching certificate, she often stepped in if the district couldn't hire a qualified teacher, or if someone was absent. I hoped she would continue in education because she obviously loved the kids.

Aisha, the middle child, was the firecracker and the center of attention. From that first weekend, Aisha was the subject of teasing and funny stories. "No! Don't tell that story!" she would protest dramatically. "For the love of God, stop! I can't take it!" A student in the Applied Communications department at the Higher Colleges of Technology Women's College in Fujairah, where Cindy also worked, Aisha was a budding filmmaker. Her first short film, "Super GambooƐa," had been selected for the 2011 Abu Dhabi Film Festival. It was the story of a young girl who thought the perfect *gambooƐa*, a large hair clip worn by Emirati girls to create the illusion of a huge pile of hair under their *shayla,* would give her super powers. Aisha was working on an idea for a second short film, for submission to the 2012 Abu Dhabi Film Festival. It would be a documentary about the children of mixed Emirati and foreign couples.

Faisal didn't talk as much as the girls did but I did learn that he was interested in mechanical engineering, and was entering a high school robotics competition. Being a boy, he enjoyed more freedom than the girls and was out playing soccer with his friends most of the time.

All three loved American fast food. Hamburgers, Subway sandwiches, and Baskin Robbins were frequent requests. It was summer, and like many Emiratis, they stayed up into the wee hours of the morning, ordering their "dinner" of burgers or pizza to be delivered in the middle of the night, and then sleeping late into the day.

A few days before my July trip, Cindy called to say that we were invited to a July 4th barbecue at an American co-worker's house. "I've never been to a Fourth of July party in the UAE before," she said. "So just to let you know – we're supposed to wear something red, white, and blue." I didn't have any star-spangled clothing, so I packed a white skirt, blue top, and red sandals.

I needn't have bothered. Cindy had not one but two identical t-shirts with heart-shaped American flags that she had brought back from one of her trips home to the U.S. I wore one with my long white muslin skirt, which I had brought thinking it would feel comfortable with the other women in their long dresses and *abayas*. Aisha wore the other shirt under her *abaya*. All three, Cindy, Aminah, and Aisha, had special American-themed *abayas* with red, white, and blue trim. The party was great fun, with a fully loaded potluck table featuring barbecued burgers and chicken, pies and cakes decorated with the American flag, and the house decorated to the hilt. It was one of the best July 4th parties I've ever been to.

Cindy and I spent three days talking, and I recorded our conversation. I learned how she met and fell in love with Mohammed in the U.S., came to live in Khorfakkan as a young, inexperienced small-town southern Baptist girl, and made a life for herself. She raised a family and became a fixture in the community, a person of importance and value, a resource. When she first arrived, she was known because of who she was – the American wife. Now she is known for what she does.

Starting this project, it was soon obvious that I needed to learn more than I'd ever thought I wanted to know about not just one religion, but two – Islam and Baptist Christian. It is impossible to tell Cindy's story without an understanding of these two religions and the links between them. Although I have researched and read, the references to religion and any description of religious practices in this book are anecdotal to the story of Cindy and Mohammed. I make no claim to be an expert on religion, nor do I wish to pass judgment on anyone's religious beliefs. There are many sources of information about Islam and

Christianity, and if you want to know more I encourage you to discover them.

Virtually all the events in this book are true, in that they are a retelling of stories that Cindy related to me. I spent five years constructing a timeline of her life and a context in which to tell her story, and she reviewed and commented on drafts. A few times she asked me to change a name to protect the identity of a person, or change or clarify a detail. Most of the people and events in this book are represented much as they were in her life, to the best of my knowledge and her memory.

Likewise, some conversations are based upon the words that Cindy spoke as she recalled them to me in her retellings, and others, I have invented as they might have occurred. The same with physical details and activities. Where Cindy left off, I invented and interpolated based on my own experience living in the UAE. There is precious little information about the early years of the UAE, and most is anecdotal. Thus, this book makes my best, although surely flawed, historical representation of the 30-year timeframe of this book.

This story is told almost entirely from Cindy's point of view because, with very few exceptions, she was my sole source of information about the events in her life. There are a few reasons for this. First, except for Mohammed's mother – and she did not speak any English – I did not meet any of Mohammed's Emirati family. Why I didn't meet them is hard to say except that, at the time, as an American woman peering into their lives, it just didn't seem possible. Also, I did not meet any of Cindy's American family. Whenever Cindy was in the USA during the past five years and I might have gone to North Carolina to meet her family, circumstances there made it inappropriate for me to insert myself and start asking questions. Finally, as much as I would have liked to, and as much as I talked about it, I never did interview Mohammed. It just never felt right to ask him questions about his marriage. As I thought about it I decided that, for the sake of time, clarity, and my fundamental purpose for this book – which was to tell the story from Cindy's point of view – I had gotten everything I needed. Maybe once this book comes out, and some of those people read it, there will be a second edition – *inshallah.*

In the end, I alone am responsible for the content of this book, its accuracy, and its message. I hope that the reader will see it for what it is intended to be – a window into life in the Middle East, the true story of a very young American woman who took a very great leap of faith.

Anne Schreiber Thomas
March, 2017

Chapter 1: Tears and Sandwiches

1982

Oh, dear God. Please. Don't let me cry.

They were sitting on the floor. The cushions, bright red stripes with bands of geometric patterns in black and white, were like the ones Mohammed had in his house. Cindy had yet to realize how common this traditional Bedouin weave was for the *majlis* – Arabic for "living room." The ladies wore flowing dresses and colored scarves, draped over their heads and wrapped around their shoulders. Speaking Arabic, they laughed and chattered to each other, glancing at Cindy, then looking away to gossip among themselves. As she stifled the urge to cry, Cindy found herself fighting an equally powerful urge to laugh. They were like birds. She imagined brown wrens, goldfinches, blue jays. Cackling like crows, they constantly adjusted their shawls as if flapping their wings. Their voices blended with the jangling of gold bracelets as they moved.

How those cushions were begging her to settle her exhausted body down. She wanted to join the ladies – they were called *ladies* here; not *women.* She turned to Mohammed's brother, Abdulrahman. He had produced an overstuffed armchair for her to sit on, apart from and looking upon this flock of new relatives from a perch above.

"I don't want to sit in this chair," she told Abdul. "I want to sit with them, on the floor."

"Never mind, don't worry," he said. "You are honored American guest. You sit in the chair."

"But, I don't *want* to sit in this chair." He didn't understand. He was Arab, and it was unthinkable for him to welcome her in any but the most gracious and hospitable way. The chair was an honor that she could not refuse.

Sighing in frustration, she turned back and met the eyes of Mohammed's mother, tiny as a child, regarding her coolly. Zamzam had politely welcomed Cindy when their plane arrived at the airport in Dubai, but there was no mistaking it: her mother-in-law did not regard her with any warmth. She would not be taking Cindy under her wing. Her small stature alone prevented that. Still, Cindy wanted to be sitting with them, to begin to feel like one of them as they chattered away, laughing and asking questions.

Under normal circumstances, this would be a ladies-only gathering, but today Mohammed's brother Abdulrahman, who spoke English, was there to translate. Cindy suddenly thought of Mohammed, already gone back to duty on the army base in Abu Dhabi. Cindy could still hardly believe it. Mohammed. He was her husband.

I'm a wife.

"America!" the ladies were passing the word from one to the other, in their Arab tongue. *Am-er-EEEK-ah.* They wanted to know how long the trip was. Which city she was from – New York or Chicago? Did they not know that not all Americans live in big cities? Hadn't Mohammed told them that she was from a small town? What *had* he told them about her?

For that matter, what had he told *her* about *them*? And this place? Not much that she could remember. She knew that Muslim women were expected to dress modestly, covering their bodies and heads whenever they were in the presence of a man who was not a close relative. A lady could remove her headscarf in the presence of her husband or father, a brother or a son. This was why they covered their heads – and some their faces – in the presence of Abdulrahman. Cindy looked more closely at them, trying not to stare. The old women were wearing strange looking masks made of leather, with a pointy beak-like nose piece and, below that, another piece that covered their lips. The mouth cover reminded her of a bad fake mustache, a thought which threatened to convulse her with a stifled giggle. She was going to either burst out laughing or melt into tears, she thought desperately.

She was tired. Too tired to smile. Too tired to speak. Never mind, they surely had never heard of North Carolina. How could she describe the mountain laurel, blooming in the spring when Mohammed had come back to get married? The lush green of the summer silver bell and witch-hazel in all their leafy glory? The fiery fall, when the elm and mulberry glowed yellow, amber, and citrine, when the dogwoods and white ash went crimson and scarlet?

North Carolina was half a world away. Cindy felt a stab of homesickness and something else, maybe fear. Could they ever understand her, who she was, and why she was there? Did she understand it yet, herself? She was a rare bird in this flock, a little American bluebird in jeans and a peasant blouse. They were fascinated with her light skin and auburn hair, flecked with summer highlights. This was their first look at her – and her first look at them. It was up to her to learn to know them, and to find a way to let them know her. The youngest of the group, a cousin of Mohammed and Abdul's, approached her, giggling, put a hand on Cindy's shoulder, touched her fine, silky hair.

"Ahlan wa sahlan."

"Welcome," Abdulrahman dutifully translated. "*Shukran* is 'Thank you.'"

Cindy managed a smile. "*Shukran.*"

It was getting late; the house was growing dim. Cindy heard a lonesome, singsong chant echoing outside the walls of the house. The sound drew her up, drew her in.

"It is the *adhan,*" Abdulrahman said. "The call to end the fast and go to pray."

"It's beautiful," Cindy said.

"It comes from the mosque. Many mosques, all around us," he said, as it faded and died.

Coffee, tea, and dates arrived. Auntie Fatima, matron of the house, served her guest first, pouring aromatic liquid from a long-spouted brass pot into a tiny porcelain cup just big enough for a mouthful or two. She smiled warmly and murmured something in Arabic as she offered the cup.

"It is Arabic coffee," Abdulrahman said. As Cindy took a gulp, and almost choked on the bitter, dry-tasting brew, the room erupted in laughter. She looked at the cup. This pale brown liquid wasn't coffee. It looked like tobacco juice. She reached out to put it down, only to have it refilled. Horrified, she turned to Abdul.

"Never mind, you will get used to it," he smiled. "It is cardamom. Not like other coffee. Do this," he held his cup and shook it, as if ringing a bell. "It means, 'No more.'" Cindy shook her cup, and the ladies smiled and nodded.

The tea was much more to her liking – warm, flowery and sweet. If it were iced tea, it would be just like the Southern sweet tea she dearly loved. Another pang of homesickness hit as she imagined sitting on the porch and sipping a tall glass of iced sweet tea with her mother. Cindy tried to eat the sticky, sweet dates that were offered, but they seemed to get stuck in her throat. Oh, how exhausted she was.

After eating a few dates and drinking a cup of tea, Abdulrahman rose. Most of the ladies rose as well, nodding at Cindy and quickly vanishing into the back of the house. "They go to pray," Abdul said. "I pray at the mosque. I will be back soon."

Cindy looked at the young women remaining before her, wondering why they, too, weren't going to pray. They giggled, talked, shook their heads, and talked more. They obviously understood her confusion, but there was no way to ask, no way to communicate.

Why am I here? she thought. *I want to go home.*

Within ten minutes all the ladies were back, and Abdulrahman was not far behind. "Why didn't everyone go to pray?" Cindy asked.

"They have their menses," he answered matter-of-factly.

"Oh!" Cindy blushed. The ladies clamored to know what had been said, and Cindy could feel herself flush almost purple as he told them. They smiled and tittered. She shook her head, trying to fight it, but she could feel the tears coming again.

She thought of Mohammed, and felt a rush of something that was new, delicious, maddening. Her husband. She longed for his soothing presence, his kind eyes full of love and secrets, his smile, his funny English. His arms that held her only in private, where no one else could observe them. How many days until those arms would surround her again? Too many.

And then, it was all too much. She hadn't slept well in over a week. She was exhausted, confused, and frustrated. She wanted to go home. And now, the last thing she wanted, was happening. The tears. She was willing them back, but they were brimming, sliding out of the corners of her eyes, hotter and more bitter than the Arabic coffee that she had just choked down. The more she fought them, the more determined they grew.

Damn. Tears. Dear God, please help me. Make them stop.

Seeing her distress, Abdulrahman quickly diagnosed the trouble. "Forgive me!" he said. "You are hungry! You need to eat."

"No! I'm not hungry – I – "

"No problem! Come, I get you American food."

"No, thank you. I don't want to eat – I just want to go home." Her room in Mohammed's house was her refuge, her only place of peace and privacy. Away from the curious eyes, the words she didn't yet understand, the constant presence of strangers. If she could only get there, she could sleep.

But Abdulrahman would not hear it. When an Arab decides that a guest must be fed, she shall be fed. Cindy was driven to the Holiday Inn – the only western hotel in the region. Food was ordered. Too tired to be hungry, jet lagged without knowing what jet lag was, she watched as a mountain of sandwiches on a large silver platter was placed before her. Chicken salad, tuna, sliced turkey, roast beef – it was enough for a dozen people.

"I don't know what you like," Abdul explained, "so I get one of each."

"*Shukran.*" Cindy murmured shyly, and then followed it with "Thank you," in English. She ate a few bites, enough to satisfy Abdul. Then thankfully, blessedly, it was time to go home.

Chapter 2: Breaking the Rules

1980

Although she wouldn't stand out in a crowd, Cindy Lou Davis possessed a delicate kind of Southern beauty. Her deep auburn hair and large, dark brown eyes contrasted with perfect, porcelain skin. A sharp little nose matched her sharp mind and betrayed a stubborn streak. She had unusually vivid cherry colored lips, a shy smile. People thought she wore lipstick; she never did. She didn't need it. It was a natural asset that God and nature had given her, along with the tiny hourglass figure that she intended to keep.

The boys in Mocksville didn't notice. She didn't have a boyfriend, not since the first one had broken her heart, but she had lots of friends. The Davises were prominent in their small North Carolina community, and Cindy's social life revolved around school and church.

Mocksville was the quintessential small town. Everybody knew everybody else and their business. It boasted the Davie County courthouse, the county library, and several well-tended cemeteries with graves dating back to the eighteenth century. One of these held the final resting place of the parents of America's greatest frontiersman. Daniel Boone himself never lived in Mocksville, but never mind; the town made the most of the fact that his parents chose to live out their days and be laid to rest there for all eternity. The Daniel Boone Festival kicked off the summer at the end of May, followed by Flag Day in June, the Main Street parade and fireworks of the 4th of July, and the county fair on Labor Day weekend. Cindy loved events, big and small. She baked cakes and cookies and made crafts for school events and church bazaars. She was hardly ever bored; there was always something to do. Mocksville was home, and she couldn't imagine living anywhere else – almost. Every so often, when she did imagine it, it was Texas. It was one of those strange things a person couldn't explain. El Paso. For some reason, it sounded like a place she'd like to live.

Cindy liked school and was good at math. It was senior year, and people were asking about her plans. Everyone in Mocksville graduated from high school, but not all could afford to go to college. Cindy planned to go to a community college for a couple of years, and on to the university and get a degree in – something. But Mocksville didn't have a community college. She'd have to leave home, which meant moving to Charlotte, and she'd have to work to pay her own way through. The kids whose parents were doctors or lawyers or professors had the money for college, but Cindy came from a large, middle-class family. Roy Davis – known to his wife and everyone else as R.G. – worked for a trucking company and Gladys was a homemaker, raising two daughters, Linda and Cindy, and four rowdy boys. Linda, the oldest, had married young. It was a shotgun wedding, and the bullet had gone straight through Gladys's heart. It was ten years already, and the marriage had lasted, but not without some troubles. Cindy knew that her mother would never get over the disappointment. Cindy was the fourth child, sandwiched in between her two pairs of brothers, and she knew that Gladys had high hopes pinned on her younger daughter. She wanted to be the antidote to the pain that Gladys had suffered. She would never want to cause her any more.

Cindy accomplished her goal by being the perfect daughter. It was her nature to try to please – although, mind you, she wouldn't be pushed around. She was spunky, opinionated, and she wouldn't be outdone, but she was never disobedient. She was the little girl people called an "angel" who grew up to be the teacher's pet – soft spoken, polite, liked and loved by everybody who knew her. But she had her own ideas, and didn't mind letting them be known. She was a sugar-coated firebrand – when she got hot about something, that sugar would burn right off.

Growing up playing rough-and-tumble with her brothers, Cindy knew how to deal with boys, how to stand up for herself. Through them, she learned how to fix things – mechanical things, wooden furniture, even plumbing and electrical. She fought back against their taunts, and as they grew older it was Randy, a couple of years younger than Cindy, to whom she was closest, and who became her defender and champion.

A few months before graduation Cindy's best friend Felicia came to her with a request. "There's a business school in Charlotte, and I want to go and check it out. I need you to go with me."

"I don't think so," Cindy said. "I don't want to go to business school."

"You're good in math," Felicia pointed out. "You could go into accounting. You'd do really great at this school." That was true, but no.

"I don't want to study accounting. I don't like it." It would be boring. Business school was a dead end. She wanted a university degree.

"You don't have to go there," Felicia wheedled. "It's just, I'm scared to go alone. Once I get there I'll be fine. But I need you to come with me. Please …" Cindy hated to say no. Maybe she should look. What would it hurt?

"Oh, all right."

They went during Easter vacation, arriving in a city that had died and come back to life. After the textile mills closed, Charlotte had gone downhill. It wasn't the kind of place that people like the Davises were inclined to visit. Now things were changing, partly because of a new law allowing alcoholic drinks to be served by the glass. Bars, restaurants and hotels were springing up. Banks and businesses had moved to town, bringing families to the brand-new housing developments popping up on the outskirts of town. The airport was expanding. Skyscrapers were going up. The Democrats were planning to hold their national convention there. It was exciting.

The business school campus was lovely, with student housing overlooking a small park, awash with crimson and pink azaleas. There was an international language school there, as well. Listening to the fast-talking woman in the registrar's office describe the accounting program, Cindy began to consider it.

"We get you in and out really quick. It's a two-year program but it's accelerated, so you start on the first of July. The other colleges don't start until September, you know, but with this one here you don't waste all that time doing nothing all summer." She could start right away.

"How long's it take to get the degree?"

"You'll be out of here and working in ten months."

Ten months. Wow. The woman was selling it, of course. She was pitching it hard, trying to get her to sign up. But it was beginning to seem like a good idea, even if it was accounting. It was not a degree, but she would get a diploma. Once she got the diploma, she could work and save some money, and then go back to school. She could still get the college degree. It would just happen a little bit later.

Maybe this was it, then, the reason why she had decided to come with Felica. This school was the answer. God was telling her something. She didn't like accounting, but sometimes what you didn't like turned out to be good for you. The thing you don't want is the thing you need. She signed up for the accounting program.

They moved to Charlotte together, two shy country girls moving to the city. Cindy and Felicia were best friends, roommates, and inseparable. During the week, they spent their time going to class and hanging out with the other girls in their dorm. Most weekends, they went home to Mocksville.

In Charlotte, there were three simple rules:

1. Don't go anywhere by yourself.
2. Always have each other's back.
3. *Don't talk to the Arab guys!*

The foreign students at the language center next to the business college were from all over the world, and a great many were Arab. Oil in the Middle East had changed their countries and their lives, and they were there to learn English, the language of business, and then go home to work in developing industries. The students were mostly – if not exclusively – men. They dressed in Western clothes, but they were distinctly Arab with their thick accents, wavy black hair, mustaches, and dark skin. They hung around together in large groups. They smelled of perfume.

They were terrifying.

When Cindy and Felicia walked between the business and language school campuses, they always had to walk past Arab guys. Eager to strike up a conversation, supposedly to practice their English, they tried to get the girls to stop. "Hello! How are you?" "Excuse me! Can I speak with you? What is your name?" But their words came out quickly, without pause, and their overtures became long, rapid, nearly unintelligible sentences: "Hellohowardyou? Whazzdyourdname? Wheredyougoing? Hello!hello!"

"Don't talk to them," Cindy and Felicia warned each other. "They're just trying to pick us up. Walk on by, and act like you don't hear them." And they would try not to smile.

Cindy did well in the program, although she didn't like accounting. It was easy, but boring. But they were using hand-held calculators, which were fascinating. She loved to play with hers, punching in numbers, hitting operation keys, and watching the electronic display change to produce an answer that would have taken her an hour to figure out on paper. One day, Cindy fumbled and dropped her calculator on the floor. It flew apart, revealing the green circuit board.

"Wow, look at that," she breathed when she saw the little pins and wires. Everything was so tiny, so complicated. It was like opening a jewelry box, only more interesting. "That is cool."

Somebody sitting nearby said, "You are in the wrong program, Cindy. You should be in computer science." But she'd already started the accounting and she wasn't about to switch now. If you started something, you should finish it.

Summer blended into fall. The air cooled, the leaves around campus blushed, faded, and fell. Living on their own, the two timid country girls bloomed into confident young women, meeting people from other places like New York, Chicago – and the Middle East.

They began talking to the Arab guys, acting friendly yet remaining cautious. They couldn't avoid it forever; these guys were everywhere. The girls would answer their questions, which were polite and harmless. Sometimes they'd even linger a bit and talk. Felicia was the first to agree to a date. After the walk around campus and a stop in a coffee shop, she told Cindy, "There's no such thing as meeting one Arab.

You meet him, you meet all his friends, and there are so many of them. They all hang out together." It was both nerve-wracking and thrilling to be pursued. They were so different than the boys they knew in Mocksville. What would people at home say?

Abdul was his name, and he asked Felicia for another date, this time to watch a movie at a house. All his friends would be there and Felicia pressed Cindy to come too. When Cindy balked, Felicia begged. "I need you to come with me. I don't want go alone." Cindy realized that Felicia liked Abdul, but she didn't trust him yet. "We have a pact to have each other's back. Remember?"

"All right, I'll go." Sigh. The plan was that Cindy would be introduced to someone there, but it wouldn't be a real date, just in case she didn't like him. It was just an excuse for her to be there.

The small house was crowded with dark young men in slacks and neat, button-front shirts. Abdul introduced Cindy to her date. Thank goodness it wasn't a real date, because Cindy could sense immediately that they didn't click at all. It was just – awkward. One by one, others were introduced. Each one nodded seriously, standing stiffly with hands at his sides or clasped behind his back to avoid a handshake. Although the house was crowded, they moved away to make plenty of room for the girls.

"This is Hassan Abdulla."

"I am Ahmed Al-Amer."

"That is Mohammed Ali."

"Abdul Amiri."

The greetings were all the same, and the names began to blend together. Everyone had two names, but she could only catch the first one, if that. Saeed. Mohammed. Faisal. Mohammed. Abdul. Mohammed. Mohammed. Mohammed. Mohammed – at least half of the guys were named Mohammed. And more kept arriving, until the place was packed with people sitting on the couches, on the floor. Every single space in the room occupied.

Cindy stayed close to Felicia, grateful for the generous space that the horde of young men left them. They seemed genuinely glad to have the two American girls in their midst. They were all polite, respectful, and gracious, continually offering them sodas, popcorn, chips, and candy. Someone turned on the television, and Saturday Night at the Movies began. This week's movie was *The Amityville Horror*. The room grew quiet, all eyes on the house with devilish eyes.

The movie couple were newlyweds. "I just wish that all those people hadn't died here," the wife said. "A guy kills his whole family? Doesn't that bother you?"

"Sure, but … houses don't have memories," the husband replied.

A chorus of *La-la! La-la!* No! No! and Yes! Yes! erupted from the assembled crowd. The audience did not agree with the husband.

"Is bad *jinn,"* Abdul told the girls. "Angry *jinn*. Something bad happen here." A priest blessed the house as the couple moved in. The Arab audience murmured their approval. "We have same," Abdul said, "to make *shaytan* go out of house." The guys were loving it.

Looking across the room, Cindy noticed someone new sitting on the sofa. "Who's that over there?" she asked Felicia. He wasn't as big as some of the others, but he had a nice face, with a neatly trimmed mustache. Handsome. But then, most of them were handsome.

"Oh, I don't know," Felicia answered, shrugging. "Some friend of Abdul's. I don't know him. There's a lot of them here that I haven't seen before." As they turned their attention back to the movie, Cindy stole another look.

Two weeks later, the girls were sitting in the little circular park near the student housing, studying. It was a pretty day in March, sunny and warm, and people were out walking. "I forgot to bring a book," Felicia suddenly said, getting up and heading for the dorm. "I'll be right back."

Alone, Cindy bent her head to study. Presently, she became aware of a car driving slowly around the circle. As it made the loop, and made it again, she realized: *That car's been circling around for a while.*

When she looked up, the car slowly came to a stop, and a guy stepped out. Cindy recognized him. It was that guy. The one at the house, sitting on the sofa, watching the movie.

"Excuse me. Were you at the house?" he asked.

"Um, yes ..."

He was just slightly taller than her five feet four. He had dark skin, dark hair, and dark eyes like all the others, but there was something different about him. He wasn't intimidating. Not at all. She liked his face. His eyes had a kindness and a twinkle. His smile wasn't dazzling, but it was familiar, reassuring. It was the smile of a man, not a boy.

"May I sit with you?" he asked.

"Well, all right, I guess."

"My name is Mohammed Ali."

Mohammed Ali! She almost laughed.

"What is your name?"

"Cindy. Cindy Lou Davis."

"It is very nice to meet you, Cindy Lou Davis."

Questions. Where was she from? Where was Mocksville? What was she studying? Did she like accounting? Gradually, the questions became more personal. What things did she like to do? Did she like discos? Did she want to go to a disco?

"No, I don't go to discos," Cindy said. Her Independent Baptist church was against it. Music and dancing were the work of the devil – although Cindy didn't think it was that bad. Even going to a movie theater was frowned upon. Cindy went to church, but it was hard for a girl her age to abide by all the rules, and to avoid everything that was supposed to be sinful. She loved country music. Despite the church's teaching, the Davises listened to Dolly Parton and other country stars. But a disco? That was out of the question. "I'm not interested in discos," she said.

"Do you smoke?" he asked. "Do you want a cigarette?"

"No!" Cindy scoffed. "I don't smoke." Smoking was a vice. Bad for the body.

"Do you drink alcohol? Do you want to go to a bar?"

What? Cindy raised her chin, and her voice – not in volume, but in pitch, as she always did when she was irritated or on the defensive. Nobody in Mocksville drank. It was still a dry county. She didn't know one single person who drank. Her words came tumbling out in a rush, one on top of the other. "NO. I have never drank alcohol. Never have and never will. Why are you even asking me that?"

"You don't drink alcohol?" Mohammed said, his eyes glinting with humor. "Are you sure you are American?"

He's teasing me. Testing me. Trying to get a reaction.

"Yes, I'm American," she retorted. "Not all Americans drink alcohol, you know. I don't do these things. I've never been to a disco. I've never drank alcohol. I've never smoked. Never did anything like that, and I never will."

He'd gotten her dander up, but she had to admit to herself that they seemed to be hitting it off, a little. She was starting to like him.

"Listen, would you like to go to dinner with me?" Mohammed suddenly asked.

That was quick. "Well. I – I guess so. All right."

"Tonight. I know a good place. Indian. Unfortunately, if Charlotte had Arab food, I would take you." Mohammed said.

The restaurant was a completely new experience for Cindy, more exotic than any place she'd been, or anything she'd ever tasted. Ethnic restaurants were starting to appear in Charlotte, but there was no such thing in Mocksville. They had Hardee's restaurant and a couple of coffee shops. That was it. There was nothing foreign there; not even a Mexican or a Chinese.

"When Felicia and I first came here," Cindy admitted, "we swore to each other that we wouldn't talk to any Arab guys."

"I can't believe it," Mohammed said. "Why?"

"We were too scared."

"Let's hope so. Surely you know we eat our young?" Cindy shook her head and laughed. This Mohammed Ali was anything but scary.

He did all the ordering, and the food kept coming.

"Please, go ahead," he kept saying. "Please, help yourself." They had an appetizer platter with pieces of chicken, dipped in a batter and fried, and little pastries stuffed with potato and green peas called *samosas*. There was grilled cauliflower, and bright orange-red *tandoori* chicken. She wanted to like the food, but everything was spicy. Finally, the waiter brought a platter of meat and vegetables in a yellow sauce that Mohammed said was curry, and he spooned some over a pile of rice and slid the plate over to Cindy. She tasted it, and sucked her breath in, hard.

"Oh, my goodness," she said, fanning her mouth with her hand. "It's so spicy! My mouth is on fire."

"My goodness! On fire!" Mohammed said, loud enough to turn the heads of nearby diners. "Take it easy! Do you want me to call the fire department?"

Now they were both laughing, eyes meeting across the table.

Chapter 3: Good News and Bad News

1981

They were dating. Suddenly Cindy had a boyfriend, and she was amazed that they'd hit if off so fast. Mohammed Ali was from a country she'd never heard of, the United Arab Emirate. He called it "UAE." He told her that Khorfakkan, the small town he was from, was by the sea, but there were mountains there too. He was in the army, studying pre-engineering at a technical school in the UAE, and was studying English in the United States on a government scholarship. That was all Cindy could find out from him. He didn't talk about home, other than to say that he had two brothers who lived in Khorfakkan and his parents lived there too.

They took walks, watched movies, hung around with his friends, drank coffee (him) and tea (her), went to restaurants, and laughed at jokes that developed between them, usually about some silly misunderstanding over the turn of a phrase, or perhaps something that they saw differently. Mohammed was always ready to poke gentle fun at himself or at Cindy. When they went out to a restaurant, he always ordered too much food. Cindy, who was a petite size four and wanted to stay that way – she would never gain weight like her sister Linda had – didn't want to eat that much food. Yet she hated to waste.

"Why'd you have to order so much food all the time? Can't we order less? We can only eat about half this."

But Mohammed insisted, using one of his newly acquired American expressions: "First, I am not a cheapskate." And then he teased her. "You do not eat enough. A baby eats more than you." And, "You are too thin. What if you get sick? You will die in one day." It was a cultural trait; she saw it when they were with his friends. There was always far more food than they needed, in case guests arrived and needed to be fed. No one would go hungry.

The weekends at home, away from Mohammed, were becoming longer and longer. Gladys noticed a change in her daughter. "Why are you moping around here?" she asked one afternoon as they were cooking supper.

"Well. As a matter of fact, I met somebody in Charlotte. I really like him. His name is, um – Mohammed."

Gladys looked up from the stove. "Mohammed? An Arab?"

"Yes. He goes to the language school."

"He's – Muslim?"

"Yes. We've been going out for a few weeks now, and I really like him." Cindy took a deep breath. "I want to invite him home next weekend. I want you all to meet him."

Gladys was silent, and Cindy rushed on. "He's really funny, and smart and very nice. And – I like him. A lot. I want you to meet him," she repeated, then held her breath.

"I'll discuss it with your father, and then we'll talk about it after dinner," Gladys said, picking up the spoon and resuming her stirring.

Cindy was nervous all throughout dinner, but determined that her mother and daddy should meet Mohammed. Almost desperate. As the weeks had worn on, and they'd spent more and more time together, it made sense, crazy as it seemed. When they were apart, she couldn't get him off her mind. When they were together, it was like heaven. They didn't touch each other except to hold hands, and perhaps exchange the shyest of kisses, but even that sent electricity down to the soles of her feet. She had to bring him home and get everyone's reaction. Then, at least, she would know what she was dealing with.

Gladys talked to R.G., and they agreed. They had better meet this Mohammed. "If you like him, Cindy, then we are happy to meet him," they told their daughter. "We'll have one of the boys give up his bed."

Randy and Cindy's other brothers thought Mohammed was cool. After all, his name was Mohammed Ali. Muhammed Ali, the heavyweight boxer, was all over the news, having come out of retirement the year before. Any American who heard the name could only think of one person. The Champ.

"Are you 'The Champ?'" they teased him. "Can we fight you?" Mohammed only laughed. He loved everything American, and he fit right in with Cindy's brothers. The five young men stayed up late that night in the family room, telling jokes and laughing.

Gladys and R.G. were friendly to Mohammed, but privately they agreed: this would never last. For God's sake, he was a Muslim, from the Middle East. They had gone to the county library and read up on it. The Encyclopedia Britannica said that a Muslim man could have up to four wives. Yet they said little about it to Cindy. In a few weeks, she would graduate from that business college, come home, and that would be that. Best to say nothing to their headstrong daughter. If they told her not to see him, she was likely to want to do the exact opposite of what they said.

Suddenly it was June. Cindy was graduating, and Mohammed was going back to the UAE. But he was coming back, he told Cindy.

"Don't worry," he said. "I'll be back before you know it, *inshallah*."

Finally, she had a boyfriend and now he was leaving. They agreed to stay in touch over the summer, but Cindy was realistic. Even if he did come back, and there was absolutely no guarantee of that, she knew that eventually Mohammed would go back to the Middle East for good, and then she would be left behind with a broken heart. He was Muslim, and they had strict customs and beliefs. She was American. She couldn't meet the standards. It just wasn't possible.

But it didn't matter because, for now, she had a boyfriend and he was Mohammed Ali. He made her laugh, he made her happy, he understood, respected, and appreciated her in a way that nobody had before. When she was with him, nothing else mattered. So what if her heart was destined to be broken? She would pick up the pieces, and then get on with her life and her college degree. It was worth it.

Then he was gone. Cindy stayed on in Charlotte, working in an accounting office, and suddenly she began to get offers for dates. College guys, Arab guys, and even local Mocksville boys were interested in her.

She sighed to herself. *Where were all these guys before I had a boyfriend?*

"Go on," Gladys urged her. "You're young. Go on out and enjoy yourself."

But she and Mohammed had an agreement. Until things changed, she would stay true to him. "I don't want to go out with anybody," Cindy told her mother. "I won't go out until I find out what happens with Mohammed. I'm going to wait until he comes back."

Even with all the fairs and festivals that were always so much fun, that summer dragged by. It wasn't easy to communicate. Long distance phone calls were expensive. Letters took so long, and often got lost, so that you might as well not send one at all. Then September arrived, but Mohammed did not. What was going on? Cindy saw Mohammed's friends around town, and one day she got up her nerve to ask.

"So, is Mohammed coming back? Or not?"

"Yes. He is coming back, *inshallah.* But there is a problem. They have taken away the money. But he is coming, *inshallah.*"

Ah, now Cindy understood all too well what *inshallah* meant. It meant "God willing," as Mohammed had explained, but it also meant a big, fat "maybe." Anything that was supposed to happen in the future would, *inshallah.* If God meant it to be. Something had changed, and Mohammed's government scholarship had been revoked. He might not be coming back to Charlotte after all, she realized. Unsure what to think, Cindy did the only thing she could think to do. She prayed to God for guidance.

Please, God, tell me what to do. Is he coming back? Should I wait for him?

Cindy thought of her high school boyfriend and their off-and-on relationship. He'd disappointed her and broken her heart again and again.

Each time he asked her to take him back, she gave in, only to be hurt again. One night she'd prayed: *Dear God, just take away this love I have for him so that he can't break my heart again.* The next time that boy came begging for her to take him back, God had answered her prayer. To her amazement, she felt nothing. The love that she'd had, that she had thought was a good thing, but was so bad for her, was gone. She even tried to get it back, just to be sure, but – nothing. It was gone forever.

Now she had this love for Mohammed, but she was sure that it was bad for her. He wasn't coming back. He was Muslim. There was no future in it. So, she decided that maybe it would work again. She would pray to God for guidance in love.

Dear God, if there is no future for this relationship, and if Mohammed is not coming back, please take away this love that I feel. I don't want this love. Please, God, take the love away so that I can go on with my life. Amen.

As the weeks turned into months, she missed Mohammed so much she thought she would go crazy. What was going on? She continued praying to God to take the love away. It only grew stronger.

Finally, one evening, the phone rang. It was Mohammed. He was back in Charlotte, and he wanted to see Cindy. At the airport they said a shy and awkward hello, and then Mohammed looked at her carefully and said, "I have good news and bad news. Which do you want to hear first?"

"I want to hear the good news," Cindy said. "And I don't want the bad news."

"The good news is – I want to get married. I want to marry you."

Married!

"The bad news," he rushed on, "is I am already married. Five years. But I am not married now."

Disbelief. But before she could think to say anything, he rushed on. "I am divorced. That is what I do in the UAE. I have four children, and I get divorce from my wife. Now I want to marry you, Cindy. I want you to be my wife."

Four children. Oh, my God. Her mind went blank. Then it began to sink in, and with it a burning sense of anger and betrayal.

She had fallen in love with him and, all this time, he had a wife and four children. How was this possible? Mohammed was only twenty-five years old. He was divorced? With children? Shock. Anger. Disbelief. How could he have kept something so important from her? He should have told her, right from the beginning. Yet if he had, she never would have dated him. Then they would never have fallen in love. That would have been better. No, it wouldn't. Oh, this thing, this love that she didn't want, it was even worse than she had thought it was. She had prayed to God to take it away, and it was still there. She had fallen in love with a married man, and he had gone away and divorced his wife. Now he wanted to marry her. How could this be what God wanted?

She had heard that customs in the Arab world were different than in America. Marriages were arranged. And she knew that a Muslim man could have more than one wife – as many as four. There were many people in Mocksville who, when they'd heard that her boyfriend was Muslim, had pointed this out. What was he asking her to do? Become a second wife? Was he really divorced?

Her mind spinning, she pulled herself back to listen to what Mohammed was saying. His marriage, he explained, had been arranged by his mother when he was young, his wife even younger. It wasn't a marriage of love, and it hadn't worked out. This kind of thing happened. It wasn't uncommon, and it was no big deal. Both families had agreed that there should be a divorce. Mohammed had gone home during the summer to get divorced and make living arrangements for his three sons and daughter. Now, with the language scholarship cancelled, he'd managed to convince the government to pay for his ticket, saying he needed to settle his affairs. He was only here temporarily, and he wasn't sure when he would get leave to come back again. But he would, *inshallah.* And when he did, he wanted to marry her.

"Please, it's ok, it doesn't matter," he pleaded. "You will come to live in the UAE but my family, they take care of the children. Everybody does this."

When she decided to go to school in Charlotte, it had never occurred to Cindy that she might find a husband instead of a career. And an Arab, someone she'd sworn never to speak to. She had never contemplated it, not when she started going out with Mohammed, and not when he left and she had pledged to be true. It was a temporary romance. A fling. A future with Mohammed had seemed so impossible. She wasn't Muslim. She was an American country girl. And what about her plans to get a degree? What about her education? What about that? If she married Mohammed, she would leave Mocksville, leave North Carolina. She had never been on a plane. Never been farther from home than right here. Charlotte.

Think.

Mohammed had four children. Cindy tried to imagine herself, a nineteen-year-old girl, as stepmother of four. This was totally crazy. And yet, there he was. Mohammed, right in front of her, with his kind eyes, handsome mustache, and arms that she desperately wanted to sink herself into. He was back in her life again after she had asked God to take him away. He was asking her to marry him. She could smell the sweet, musky perfume on his skin. She could feel his heart beating for her, as hers was beating for him. She wanted nothing more than to run away, and yet nothing seemed more impossible. Run back to life in Mocksville? There was nothing there for her, compared to what she felt for Mohammed. But everything she knew and cared about was in Mocksville. Going away with Mohammed was like leaping off the edge of the Earth. Was she willing to risk it all for Mohammed?

When Cindy and Felicia started dating Arab guys, they did it without a single thought about the future and what it might hold. It was an adventure that they couldn't guess would change their lives, take them away from home and country, and immerse them in a foreign culture far different from their roots in North Carolina. Felicia would live with one foot in the Middle East, marrying a Lebanese man but remaining in America. Cindy's choice would change her life. She felt the heat rise within her, the burning desire for this man she'd come to love. Suddenly it didn't matter what anyone else would think or say. It wasn't a choice; it was destiny. She'd prayed to God and God had answered, had strengthened her love for Mohammed, had sent Mohammed back to her. Mohammed had told her that he wasn't married any more, that he'd gotten divorced, and she believed him. Pushing her anger aside, refusing to consider how far from home and family it would take her, she gave her answer.

"Yes. Yes, I want to marry you."

Cindy's church had instilled in her a deep faith and more than anything, she believed in God's will. She trusted fate. She knew that they were meant to be. She hadn't dreamed that a small-town American girl such as herself would be good enough to be Mohammed Ali's wife, but he thought she was, and that was good enough for her. It was going to be them, together. Mohammed Ali and Cindy Lou Davis. It was all that mattered. She didn't care about anything else.

Chapter 4: Never Look Back

It was December. Mohammed went back to the UAE. It would be at least six months before the Army would grant him another leave, but he would come back and when he did, they would get married. Cindy quit her job in Charlotte and went back to Mocksville to wait, working for a local CPA and living at home.

Had she thought about it, she might have changed her mind. If she had listened to any of the many voices subtly trying to talk some sense into her head. But instead she went on living her familiar day to day life, believing that if it was meant to be, it would happen. Looking back on it years later, she would say perhaps she was too young to comprehend it. But at the time, she didn't dwell on it, didn't conjure up what-ifs. It wasn't a choice she was making. Something more basic and more powerful than conscious thought was working in her. Love. Desire. Faith. Destiny.

Cindy immersed herself in church and community. She went to the Independent Gospel Church with her family every Wednesday night and twice on Sundays. She studied the Bible. She went to movies and sat in the coffee shop, gossiping and giggling with her friends. And she decided that, if she was moving to the Middle East, she would learn the Arabic alphabet.

Again, Cindy found herself popular with boys who had never given her the time of day before. Why did they suddenly notice her now? Was there something about her that was different? Were her parents putting out the word around town, so that people would suggest to their sons to ask her out? If she'd gotten all these offers before, she thought, she would've jumped on it. But now she was engaged so it didn't matter. She wasn't available.

One boy, whose parents were friends of the family, kept asking her out. "Why don't you just go out with him?" Gladys prodded. "Go out, have some fun. Mohammed's a long way away. You're not married yet. You're young. Have some fun."

"I'm engaged, Mama. I'm not going out with him." She was trying to get Cindy to forget about Mohammed. But that wasn't going to happen.

Cindy knew what her mother was thinking. She wanted to see her daughter happy, and she wasn't at all sure about this engagement. Who was this foreign man who had stolen her heart? What would happen if he did come back, and they got married? She would be the wife of a Muslim. They would live in the Middle East. And how many other wives would he have? She tried, as often as she dared, to convince Cindy that she should go out with this or that local boy, hoping that she'd find someone who would interest her, a Christian, and then she'd forget about Mohammed. But it was no use.

It hardly felt real, but Cindy felt attached, however remotely. It was enough just to be engaged, to wait for Mohammed's rare phone calls, and to exchange the letters that took so long to arrive. To look at his picture and to show it to her girlfriends, who were far more enthusiastic than her family. As the first one in the group to get engaged, she had a new status among them, and they thrilled over every detail, few as they were. Looking at his picture, they thought Mohammed was so handsome.

"I think he looks like Tom Selleck. Look at that mustache. And those eyebrows. And he's tan, like he's from Hawaii."

"But look at this one. He looks exactly like Erik Estrada." Cindy chuckled over the idea that Mohammed had television-star looks.

By early spring, the phone calls grew fewer, the letters farther between. Then, a couple of months went by, and Cindy heard nothing. Her brothers taunted her.

"What have you heard from your boyfriend lately? Mohammed Ali? The Champ? Where is he? Is his car stuck in the desert? Is he having trouble starting his camel?" They liked Mohammed, but it didn't stop them from poking fun. Mohammed would have laughed at their jokes, if he'd been there to hear them, but Randy was the one who always said, "Stop it. Leave her alone." She only raised her chin and brushed them off, but he knew that the teasing was getting under Cindy's skin.

Around town people were still nice, but she could see that they were beginning to doubt that the engagement was real. They politely asked how it was going, and where her fiancée was, and then they would smile and nod when she said, it was fine, but he was still back in the Middle East and she hadn't heard much lately.

Some people got more to the point. "Well, you don't really want to leave Mocksville anyway, now, do you?" "What do you want to live over there for? In the Middle East?" "It's so hot there." And then the question they all asked: "Is his name really Mohammed Ali? Like, The Champ?" She got that all the time.

Cindy's well-intentioned girlfriends pressured her to go out with guys they were trying to fix her up with, and she agreed to go but only in large groups. "There's this guy, Bob, he's really nice. I want you to meet him." Cindy wasn't interested, but she felt her faith and resolve being tested. She didn't want to betray Mohammed. It had been so long, almost two months, since she'd heard anything at all from him. She didn't know what was going on. Maybe he had changed his mind. She had written, but she didn't think her letters ever reached him. There were so many that had already gotten lost in the mail. Bob turned out to be nice enough, and she agreed to a dinner that Friday with two other friends, their husbands, and kids. It was a way to get them to take the pressure off without having to go on a date.

"What about your fiancée?" Bob asked, half teasing, trying not to seem too interested.

"Ah," Cindy brushed the question off. "I haven't heard from him in months." Maybe Mohammed wasn't coming back. Maybe God was sending her someone else, after all.

On Wednesday, there was a phone call. "Cindy!" Gladys called.

It was Mohammed. "I am in New York," he said. "Come and pick me up at the airport in Charlotte in three hours. I have one-month leave. We will get married!"

And with that, after weeks and weeks without a word, Cindy knew. It was happening.

It was early June. Cindy was determined to do it right, a church wedding, with a white dress and a cake. She wanted the whole package, and she had one month to plan it. On top of that, she needed a passport. With barely enough time to get it all done, she made the guest list, sent invitations, found a wedding dress, and planned the reception, which would take place right there in the community room at the church after the wedding.

Cindy had always been close to the minister and his wife; she baby-sat their kids. When she asked him to marry her and Mohammed he agreed, but he wasn't enthusiastic. A few days later, his wife asked to meet with Cindy. "You can't do this," she said flatly. "The church doesn't allow it. Mohammed's already been married, and you can't have two wives before God. You have to show that his marriage was annulled."

When she went to Mohammed and told him, he said that it wasn't possible. That wasn't how they did it over there. The marriage was legally dissolved, not annulled. Under Islamic law marriage is a legal agreement, not a religious sacrament. There was no such thing as an annulment of marriage.

Cindy knew that the minister's wife was worried about the fact that Muslim men could have more than one wife. She probably didn't believe that Mohammed was divorced. Others had the same concerns. It seemed like everyone in the church was trying to stop her marriage.

"You're going to be living in a tent in the desert. Riding on camels."

"You'll have to convert. To become a Muslim."

"You'll have to cover yourself up with veils. You won't be allowed to go outside."

"You won't have any freedom. It will be like prison."

"You're going to be part of a harem."

She heard it over and over, what people thought they knew. What she knew, and they didn't know, was that none of this mattered because she was marrying Mohammed. He was different.

And there was always this: "How can you leave us?" Meaning, how can you leave your family, your neighbors, your church, your community? Your parents? Your mother? That was the worst of all because there was no good answer to that question. It tore at her heart. Still, all that mattered was being with Mohammed. That was the only answer. Mocksville had been enough for her until she met him. Now, she would travel across the globe for him. She would do anything to be with him. It was like she was closing her eyes and getting on the world's biggest Ferris wheel, riding to the top – and stopping. If she were beside Mohammed, she could stay there forever. Whatever should happen when they started back down, they would be in God's hands.

Seeing the creases of worry in her parents' faces caused Cindy the most pain. Gladys cried often, which made Cindy's heart ache with guilt, yet at the same time it deepened her resolve to prove to them, and everybody else, that she would be happy with Mohammed. Her father simply said, "You're marrying a nigger." That word. To R.G., it was just a word that people used. Cindy didn't like it, but she was used to it. People like her daddy, of a certain generation in a Southern town where the races remained separate, used that word to refer to someone who wasn't white. R.G. had no reason to dislike Mohammed – he liked him well enough. He had plenty of coworkers and friends who weren't white – blacks, Native Americans – and he didn't believe that they were in any way inferior to him. But he and Gladys had both been raised to believe that you marry someone of your own kind. R.G saw that Cindy was marrying someone different, someone he didn't know, someone who was not from the South, who didn't look like them, didn't do as they did. To him and Gladys, who came of age before the 1960's, marrying someone of another race just wasn't right, and this was the only way he knew how to express it. Her father's comment hurt Cindy, but she knew he didn't mean anything against Mohammed. She raised her chin, fired up to defend her decision.

"First of all, if you mean that he's black, well, he isn't," she said. "He's Arab. But what difference does skin color make? If I want to marry him, then I am going to marry him. If you don't like it, then that is your problem. Say what you like. I won't change my mind." Her father said nothing more.

What troubled Cindy more than her daddy's words was what the minister's wife had said. Was it true? Mohammed was divorced. Could they get married in the church? How could she get an annulment paper if Mohammed said it was impossible? She went to the church pastor.

"No," he told her, but not without some resignation. "It isn't true. Mohammed wasn't married in the Christian church. He was not married in God's eyes." Cindy's heart flooded with relief. They could get married in her church, after all. "You have to forgive the minister's wife," the pastor said. "She is worried about you."

Cindy knew the minister and his wife meant well. They, like everybody in her church, were doing what they thought was right by discouraging the wedding. They loved Cindy. She was their baby sitter. To the parents and grandparents of her friends, she was like one of their own kids. They saw that they were losing her. The whole town was losing her. They didn't want to let her go, didn't want her to leave the fold to marry a foreigner and go to a place far away. They feared that she would forsake her Christian beliefs and become a Muslim. There was nothing they could do to stop her. The only thing they could do was to make it harder, and try to make her aware of what she was doing. Unfortunately, this only strengthened her resolve.

Cindy's brothers already treated Mohammed like one of them, and soon he would officially be their brother-in-law. Once her father got to know Mohammed, and saw what a good person he was, everything would be all right. They would see how happy he made her. And if they couldn't see it – then that would be their problem. None of it mattered. They could all think and say what they wanted. She trusted Mohammed to make her happy, and she wanted to make him happy. This marriage was meant to be. If others didn't like it, they should just look the other way.

Cindy never told Mohammed about the date that almost was. She didn't want him to think that she had almost give up on them. But if she had told him, he would surely have said that it was God's will that they would be together, and that it was all a test from God. His phone call that Wednesday came out of the blue, and just in time. It was God's proof that marrying him was His will and her destiny. They had both known it from the start, and now there was no looking back.

Davis – Al-Hammadi Are Wed

Miss Cindy Lou Davis and Mohammed Ali Al-Hammadi were united in marriage Sunday, June 29, at 3 p.m. at Gospel Baptist Church of Mocksville. The Rev. Lee Childress officiated at the double ring ceremony.

A program of wedding music was presented by Johnny Cashwell of Advance, N.C.

The bride, escorted by her father, wore a formal gown of Victorian influence. The gown of satin and organza featured an empire waist with a v-neckline that extended upward to a sheer illusion yoke of schiffli embroidery, fitted lace sleeves, and an A-line skirt with baby doll ruffles that extended into a chapel length train. She carried a bouquet of white and blue silk flowers.

Miss Karen Hutchins of Mocksville was maid of honor. She wore a formal gown of baby blue silk and carried matching silk roses.

The bride's brother, Dale Davis, served as best man.

Mrs. Candy Davis kept the guest register.

The wedding was directed by Mrs. Betty Childress.

The bride's parents are Mr. and Mrs. Roy Davis of Route 6, Mocksville. She is a 1980 graduate of Davie High School and a 1981 graduate of Kings College, where she studied accounting.

The bridegroom is the son of Ali Mubarak and Zamzam Hassan Ahmed of the United Arab Emirates.

RECEPTION

A reception following the ceremony honored the couple and their guests in the church fellowship hall.

The refreshment table was covered with a white lace cloth, accented with blue ribbons, and centered with an arrangement of blue and yellow silk flowers.

Assisting with the serving were Mrs. Hazel Phillips and Mrs. Tammy Driver. Refreshments included a two-tiered wedding cake, bridal punch, decorated mints and mixed nuts.

Cindy (center) and siblings (clockwise from upper left) Terry, Bobby, Dale, Linda, and Randy.

Engagement photo. Cindy had the popular "Lady Di" haircut

Wedding album

Chapter 5: In a Strange Land

1982

They left North Carolina and everything familiar ten days after the wedding. The impact of her decision began to sink in as she boarded an airplane for the first time in her life – her life which was changing forever. She was about to hurtle, literally, into the unknown. She was going to some place in the Middle East called the United Arab Emirates. She would be far away from home and everything she knew. Everyone would be speaking a language she did not understand, and they would not understand hers. She would be all alone.

But no, she wouldn't. She had Mohammed by her side.

Charlotte to New York. New York to London Heathrow. Heathrow to Dubai. The plane landed at Dubai International Airport at 9 p.m. As they prepared to land, Cindy saw the golden lights of Dubai, concentrated along the coastline like one of her mother's costume jewelry pins. A cluster, with arcs radiating out into darkness. Straining to peer out the window as the plane approached the runway, she saw a smooth, flat, tan landscape, textured by tan buildings that looked like cardboard boxes with towers. A dark river punctured the coastline, ending in a bay and a cluster of skyscrapers. Glowing green spires dotted the ground beneath them.

"They are mosques," Mohammed said, "in every neighborhood. No one walks more than five minutes to prayer." As the plane few low, Cindy could see men, dressed in light-colored tunics and matching pants, gathered in groups here and there.

She was seeing a city which had grown over the course of Mohammed's lifetime from a coastal town with a modest population of 40,000, into a cosmopolitan city of more than 350,000 when Cindy arrived as a 20-year-old bride. The river was the *Khor Dubai* – Dubai Creek, a shallow natural inlet that extended inland for several kilometers, ending in a *sabkha*, or salt flat, near the airport.

"Dubai is growing," Mohammed said. "This will be a great city. One of the greatest in the world. You see nothing yet." He paused. "We will come back soon, *inshallah.* We will shop at the *souk,* and ride the *abra.* "

"What's that? *Abra?* "

"It is a boat. Down there. It crosses *Bur Dubai.* That is the *Deira.* Many shops. " Cindy saw the tiny boats out on the water, crossing the creek, landing at the docks beside barges stacked with goods.

Mohammed didn't have the English to explain the city's history to his bride. Established in the eighteenth century as a trading outpost for pearl fishermen from Abu Dhabi, Dubai town had soon become an import and trading center, attracting Persian traders from across the gulf. The original town grew up along both sides of the creek, with clusters of houses and a *souk,* or market, on the west bank. A fort was built a few hundred meters from the *souk,* but when Cindy and Mohammed arrived it had already been converted into a center for culture and heritage. Across the creek which the *abras* were busily crossing was the busy *Deira,* the commercial center where the streets teemed with men until late into the night as cafeterias and grooming salons stayed open for customers coming from evening prayer. Beyond the compact historic commercial district, shiny new skyscrapers were sprouting beside the mangroves and grasses in the *sabkha* just a few kilometers beyond. Three decades later, Cindy would look over the same landscape and marvel at its transformation.

Where the lights of Dubai ended, the world was black.

They landed on the tarmac, and waited while airplane steps were rolled out. Already, even though they were still on the plane, Cindy felt the heat radiating through the windows, stealing in through every vent. When they emerged from the plane, it threatened to strangle her. She could feel the sweat pouring into every crevice, every fold of skin. Her back was soaked within seconds. It was even hard to breathe.

"Man, this place is hot," she gasped. And this was nighttime, after the sun had gone down. What would it be like during the day?

"Of course, it is hot in summer," Mohammed said. "Cooler in October …"

October? It's only the beginning of July …

"… the end of October."

Oh, man.

Mohammed had told her that it would be hot, but not this hot. She would learn in time that summer in Dubai averaged well over 100 degrees during the day, and hovered in the 90's at night. The vast desert soaked up the sun all day, as did the shallow waters of the Persian Gulf. As the sun set, and the air cooled slightly, the result wasn't refreshing. Steamy vapor rose from the Gulf, turning the air into a cloying mixture of heat, dampness, and a thousand perfumes. The transition from sunset to darkness was like stepping from a sauna into a steam bath.

Cindy reached for Mohammed's hand as they walked from the plane to the terminal. She would be meeting his parents soon. But instead of clasping her hand as he usually did, Mohammed pulled away. She felt a stab of pain in her gut, and the first crack in her confidence. Had she made a mistake? Were things changing so soon, as people had told her they would?

"We cannot kiss or hug in public," he said. "It is forbidden. We cannot even hold hands. It is indecent in Arab countries." And then he looked at her. "Don't worry. Wait until we are alone."

With that one look, Cindy went from deflated to elated. Hand-holding in public was forbidden, but what? She was no exhibitionist. She didn't like seeing people kissing in public, all over each other. This would be fine. She and Mohammed would save their affection for private times. It would make it all the sweeter.

Mohammed's father, brother, and mother were there to greet them in the air-conditioned terminal. The men were wearing the UAE national dress, a spotlessly white ankle-length tunic that Cindy would later know as the *kandura,* starched and pressed to perfection. On their heads, they wore white cloths secured with black ropes. Those, she would eventually learn, were called the *ghutra* and *agal.* Mohammed's mother wore a flowing black cloak, and her head was covered with a shawl, which she constantly adjusted to ensure that it was completely covering her head and most of her face. Her small black figure all but vanished beside the imposing white-clad men.

While they waited for their luggage, Cindy thought about her collection of blue jeans, tops, and the few dresses she had brought. Mohammed had told her that women in the UAE wore long dresses, covering their legs, and they wore long sleeves. Were her clothes modest enough? She would probably need to get some long dresses.

Mohammed greeted his brother, and Cindy recognized the sound of the Arabic words she had heard when Mohammed greeted his friends in Charlotte. *"Al-salaam 'aalykum." "Aalykum salaam,"* his brother answered. Then, they touched noses and made a kissing noise. Mohammed then did the same with his father. Turning to his mother, he took her hands and kissed the right side of her face, then the left, and then the right again, murmuring in the same greeting in Arabic.

If Cindy had any illusions that she would be greeted with warm Western-style hugs, they were quickly dispelled. Mohammed's mother Zamzam, father Ali Mubarak, and brother Abdulrahman each greeted Cindy in turn, leaning toward her, kissing one side of her face, then the other. Then it was time to pile into the car for the drive to Khorfakkan.

The lights of Dubai faded in an instant, and suddenly the only illumination on the road was coming from their headlights. Leaving Dubai and the coastal plain, they were driving east. Despite her exhaustion, Cindy could sense that they were heading uphill. They must be going through mountains, she thought, as sleep threatened to overcome her. Then she realized that Mohammed was talking to her.

"This is brand-new road," he said. "Less than one year. Before this road is built, we take all day to drive to Khorfakkan from Dubai. We drive in the *wadi* – the river bed. Now, it is less than two hours."

They were about to cross the Hajar mountain range, the sharp, rocky spine dividing the Arabian Peninsula's western coastal plain from the east coast. Looking at the jagged peaks rising against the moonlight, Cindy couldn't imagine enduring a whole day driving, bumping along on a dirt road for hour after hour. She had one last thought, before falling asleep.

What have I gotten myself into?

More than an hour later, she opened her eyes to a splash of light. "Are we there? Is that Khorfakkan?"

"Not yet," Mohammed answered. "This is Fujairah." They passed through the city and turned north along the coastline, passing oil containers, shipping cranes and loading docks. As they sped along on the two-lane road, Cindy caught glimpses of shabby-looking buildings, dimly lit, cluttered with piles of metal or machinery. It was the middle of the night, or seemed like it, but still people were out and about.

Suddenly they were in a town. Khorfakkan. They were almost home. They slowed and turned onto a side road, the car lurching and heaving on the unpaved surface. "Man," Cindy said, "this place is rocky."

"Don't worry," Mohammed said. "Where we live it is paved."

"What – then – why aren't we going there?"

"First, we are going to my auntie's house.

Cindy was tired. She was ready for a shower. She wanted to go to bed. "Can't we get some rest, and go see them in the morning?"

Mohammed shook his head. "The family is there, waiting. They want to meet you. We must go."

"But – isn't it awfully late?"

She didn't want everyone to get the impression that Mohammed's new American wife would act spoiled and demanding. That she didn't want to meet them. If there was one thing that she already knew, had sensed and seen with Mohammed and his friends despite the lack of common language, it was that family was the center of life and that hospitality and celebration was at the center of family. The car bumped along.

"It is Ramadan," Mohammed finally said, as if that explained everything. "Holy month."

"Oh. Okay." She drew in her breath, gathered up her strength.

The women were in one room, men in another. As they arrived, the men came outside to greet Mohammed and meet Cindy. They were all dressed in identical snow-white *kanduras, ghutras,* and *agals,* the Emirati national dress, like Mohammed's brother and father. They wore sandals on their immaculately clean feet. Like Abdulrahman and Ali Mubarak, they were polite and welcoming to Cindy, but there was no touching, no handshakes or friendly pats, much less hugs. Instead, with each introduction she received a nod of the head. They received Mohammed with a nose-to-nose greeting.

Mohammed had told Cindy to remove her shoes before entering the house, but of course she forgot. The moment she got into the room, she realized her mistake. *What a way to start.* Mortified, she returned and left them outside the door with the pile of sandals, and went inside to meet the women. The first to greet her was Mohammed's Auntie Fatima, the lady of the house. What Zamzam had lacked in warmth, Fatima made up for, saying "*Ahlan wa sahlan!* Welcome!" Taking Cindy by the hands, she leaned in and kissed the air on one side of her face, then the other, and then the first side again – the greeting reserved for close family and friends. It said, "You are one of us." Others lined up, and Cindy was greeted, one by one, with a smile and a small kiss at each cheek.

After the introductions, they used Auntie Fatima's phone to call Gladys. "Hi, Mama, we made it here okay," Cindy spoke into the phone. It was the middle of the night in the UAE, but in Mocksville it was only 5 p.m.

"Cindy! It's so good to hear from you. I've been waiting for the call. How are you doing?" She could hear her call out, "R.G.! It's Cindy!"

"I'm fine, just tired. We're meeting some of the relatives right now. I can't talk long." It was expensive, although she wouldn't bring that up.

"How was your flight? Where are you now? What time is it there?"

"It was fine. We're at his auntie's. It's not that late. But we'll be going home soon." She didn't want to tell her mother that she hadn't slept in two days. It would set her to worrying even more than she already did.

"Okay, then, Honey. Well, you get some rest. You know I'm here, any time you want to call. You be sure and write, too."

"Yes, Mama, I will. Don't worry about me. I'm fine."

"Okay, then, well. 'Bye then."

"'Bye Mama." Her eyes burned as she hung up the phone. Whether it was tears or just tired eyes, Cindy didn't know.

Mohammed left Cindy with the ladies while he went to sit with the men in the other room. When he had gone, closing the door securely behind him, most of the ladies removed their head scarves, arranging them onto their shoulders. It was a taste of what her new social life would be like in the UAE. Hot sweetened tea was served, along with several kinds of dates, some bright amber, sticky and sweet, others with a mottled, flaky dry skin. There was a large basket of fruit. Green grapes, blushing mangoes, tiny bananas no bigger than a man's thumb, and a small fruit, deep pink and prickly looking. She watched one of the ladies reach for one and peel off the thick outer skin, revealing a translucent white, watery center which she popped into her mouth, removing an almond-sized seed a moment later. They kept offering things to her, but Cindy was too tired to feel hungry. And why did they drink their tea hot in weather like this? It was almost two a.m. Despite the air conditioning in the house, Cindy felt hot and clammy.

Man, she thought, *what I wouldn't do for a glass of iced sweet tea right now.*

A knock sounded, scarves went back onto heads, and the door opened for Mohammed. At long last they could get away. Finally, in their room, in his house, she could be alone with her husband, and they could sleep. As they went to bed, Mohammed gave instructions to the houseboy who, to her surprise, appeared a few minutes after they entered the house. Auntie Fatima had a housemaid, but she hadn't realized that Mohammed had a servant, as well.

"I tell him you are not Muslim. He brings you breakfast with ice tea," Mohammed told Cindy. It was Ramadan, and it was Friday, the weekly day of prayer. Muslims would be rising early for a meal before sunrise, he explained simply, and they would not eat again until after sundown. Mohammed would be gone to the mosque when she woke up, but he would be back later in the day, and they would have one precious day together. His leave was all used up. He would be going to the base the next morning.

The houseboy brought her breakfast as instructed. A pot of hot tea, a cup of ice, and bowl of Jell-O. Cindy had never eaten Jell-O for breakfast before. She would soon learn that it was one of the staple foods eaten by Muslims during Ramadan. Although it looked and tasted the same, it wasn't the Jell-O she ate at home. It was *halal* jello made from cattle or fish, instead of pork. All meat products must be certified *halal,* the animals killed per Islamic law. Cindy hadn't thought much about the food. Now, she wondered – when would she see American food again?

When Mohammed returned, they set out on a tour of Khorfakkan. Mohammed, in Emirati national dress, looked so different, so regal, that Cindy caught her breath. Was this really her Mohammed? Then he spoke.

"Ok," he said. "*Bismallah. Yalla.* Let's get going."

Perched in the back seat of the Datsun sedan were Mohammed's two young cousins, both around ten years old. They peppered Cindy with questions, practicing the English they were learning in school. "You have television in *Amer-eeeka*," the boys said. They asked her what shows she watched, but they didn't recognize any of the ones she named, nor had she heard of theirs.

"Television in UAE is not like America," Mohammed said. "We have one station, from Abu Dhabi. Not a lot of American shows. Most from Saudi Arabia, India, Japan." Cindy wondered if she would ever see any of her favorite soap operas again. How would she know what was happening with Luke and Laura on *General Hospital*? But her musing was interrupted by more chatter from the back seat.

"You are white," the boys were saying. "*Jamila. 'Abyad.* White."

"I am *not* white!" she protested. "I have a tan." Mohammed was laughing. "I worked hard on this tan, so I would fit in better here."

"Wait a minute, take it easy, Honey," he said. "White skin is pretty here. That is what *jamila* means. Anyhow, you should take it as a compliment." She might as well not have bothered trying to tan, anyway. No matter what, her skin was white even with the little bit of tan she could get.

Making their way out of the maze that was their neighborhood, Cindy saw for the first time the rugged, dusty streets of Khorfakkan. Some were paved with old bricks, some with newer ones, others with stones and sand compacted by decades, perhaps centuries, of use. The oldest houses were a helter-skelter jumble made of mud, stone, and palm leaves. Electricity was patched together with electrical wiring and extension cords. Other houses were made of plaster, clustered together behind makeshift barriers. The newest houses, like Mohammed's, were hidden behind tall concrete block walls with colorfully painted iron gates.

"Khorfakkan is not as big as Fujairah," Mohammed said. "But it is especially important port. My father is customs agent."

Mohammed was eager to explain the UAE's proud history, but the language barrier between them was great. All he could tell her was that Sheik Zayed was a great leader, was very good and generous to the people of the UAE. Over time, Cindy would learn more about her new home, and there would be books and articles to read, but in 1982 the history of the UAE was still passed down mainly through storytelling.

Khorfakkan was the second-largest town in Sharjah, one of the seven emirates, or states, of the United Arab Emirates – the UAE. Khorfakkan and its bigger neighbor, Fujairah, had been inhabited since prehistoric times, operating continuously as ports since the 15th century. A small but important port, Khorfakkan was controlled by Dutch and Portuguese traders during the 15th and 16th centuries. The ruins of forts from that era still stood. *Al Bidya,* a few miles north of Khorfakkan, was the site of the oldest mosque in the UAE, dating back to 1446.

When Cindy arrived in 1982, the UAE was just eleven years old. Earlier, the region was called the "Oman coast," or sometimes "Pirate Coast." Isolated by sand and sea for centuries, the local economy was based on tribalism and trade. In 1853 a treaty between Great Britain and the ruling sheikhs created the Trucial States, uniting the Arab sheikdoms on the Arabian Peninsula under the British. Not much changed during nearly two hundred years as a British territory. Then in 1968, Great Britain announced its intention to officially withdraw, and after three years of negotiations, the United Arab Emirates was born with the union of six of the Trucial States, a seventh joining the following year. The father and beloved leader of the UAE was the charismatic Sheikh Zayed bin Sultan al Nahyan.

Under the British, the discovery of oil in the Middle East had made little difference in the lives of the people of the Arabian Peninsula. The business of and profit from oil had been largely hidden. Now, with local control over its export and a visionary leader who imagined cities with modern infrastructure, schools, and hospitals, oil was transforming the UAE and its people, thrusting them headlong into the 20th century. It was happening at lightning speed in Abu Dhabi and Dubai, as skyscrapers rose into the sky and multistory housing mushroomed below. The port at Fujairah was expanding. Change was seeping into quiet Khorfakkan, as well.

The UAE's most dramatic and unimaginable changes were still in the future, but Mohammed's life had already changed completely. He was born in Khorfakkan, in a cave beside the sea. As a teenager, during the sweltering summers he and his brothers had slept on the roof of their palm-frond *barasti* hut, covered in wet sheets to cool them. Now, a decade later, he and nearly all Emiratis had houses with walls, windows, doors – and air conditioning.

There were no skyscrapers in Khorfakkan but, in town, the main street's concrete shops were multiplying, filling with immigrant shopkeepers and tradesmen ready to make a living in newly declared professions. Building contractors, plumbers, electricians, and appliance sales and repair shops occupied new blocks next to long-established mechanics, welders, grocers, butchers, textile merchants, tailors, sandal makers, tent makers, and men's and ladies' grooming salons.

Because she had memorized the Arabic alphabet, Cindy could read the signs, although she didn't know what they meant. *HALAQ* (barber) – *KHIAT* (tailor) – *LIHAM* (welding) – *ALMANSUJAT* (textiles) – *MATEAM* (restaurant) – she read them all as they flew by, but it was gibberish to her.

There was one place, in the heart of town, where the meaning of *ALSSINAMA* on the marquee was clear. "That's a movie theater, isn't it?" Cindy asked. "What movies do they show there? Do you ever go? Could we go there sometime?"

"No way, it's impossible. It is Indian movies," Mohammed said. "The place is only for men. Ladies don't go there."

Where the commercial district ended, the road became a shoreline drive that Mohammed called the *corniche*. As Cindy caught her first glimpse of the Gulf of Oman, on the great Indian Ocean, she caught her breath. Dazzlingly bright topaz water lapped at a white sand beach. After the grim, gritty, dusty town, the scene was so gorgeous it was almost surreal.

"Oh, it's so beautiful," she breathed. To their right, between the road and the beach, stretched a grassy strip with shaded picnic areas with swing sets for the children. Even with the shade, the midday heat was too overwhelming for anyone to be out.

"People come out later," Mohammed said, "after the sun goes down. Some people stay out all night during Ramadan. Night owls." Another expression he'd learned in America.

To the left, across the road from the beach, was a line of gleaming houses painted white and beige, facing the sea against a stunning backdrop of the steep, rugged Shumayliyah mountain range. The crescent shaped shoreline stretched away to the north for five miles, ending at a hotel-topped peninsula. Further up the coast, the Hajar mountains found their way to the sea on the Musandam Peninsula.

Pointing toward the cheery looking houses, Cindy said, "I want to live in one of those!"

Mohammed's response was immediate, firm, and automatic. "No. You cannot live there."

"Why not? It's so pretty here."

"It is too far away. You must live with family."

"What do you mean, it's too far away? It's only a few blocks." It seemed ridiculous. Too far away from the relatives? Why, she could easily walk that far, and besides, soon she'd get a car and then she could drive anywhere. "Why? Why can't I live here?"

"It is not possible. You do not understand. There are no neighbors. You cannot live by yourself."

Then, she realized what Mohammed was saying. It would be unacceptable for her to live alone while he lived on base during the week. This was Arabia, where daughters lived with their parents until marriage and if the husband was away, they stayed under the wing of relatives. This was not the USA, where Cindy could leave home with her girlfriend Felicia to go to business school, or work a job and live in an apartment. What had seemed so normal at home was unheard of here, where every decision was a family decision, every occasion was a family event. Cindy must remain a few steps away from them, where everyone would know what she was doing. In this world, there was no such thing as independence for women, at least not as Cindy understood it. What she did was everyone's concern. That was the way things were.

Despite the time he had spent in the USA, Mohammed was an Arab, an Emirati, and he came from a small conservative town. He cared deeply what his family thought, what they said. Cindy would learn, eventually, that to all outside eyes Arab men called the shots, yet the women, while legally subordinate to their husbands, wielded their own subtle kind of power. For now, Mohammed was right. Cindy didn't understand. Not yet, but soon she would.

"*Inshallah,* when I have money, we will move to Abu Dhabi," Mohammed said. "It is bigger. You will like Abu Dhabi. Now, I have no money. I have divorce, and houses to pay for. I need time. Please, Honey, be patient." Not only was he paying for his own house but, as the eldest son in the family, he was helping other family members financially. As first born son, Mohammed was responsible for the welfare of the entire family. It was his obligation to take care of the children from his first marriage, his parents, and his two younger brothers. If anything went wrong, if anyone needed help, it was Mohammed's duty to step up.

Suddenly Cindy realized what this meant. She would not have her own place. She would live in Mohammed's house, which he shared with his brothers, within walking distance of Zamzam and Ali Mubarak and the rest – aunties, uncles, cousins. That was all there was to it. They would watch over her during the week, in Mohammed's absence. Until they moved to Abu Dhabi, whenever that might be – maybe a year? two? – Cindy would see Mohammed only on the weekend, which was one day. Friday. The other six days of the week, she would live in Khorfakkan with the relatives while Mohammed lived on base near Abu Dhabi. All week, she would wait for Mohammed to come home for that one day.

She and Mohammed had spent more time apart than together during their engagement, and now their marriage would start off the same way. The months of separation, waiting anxiously, had prepared her to be Mohammed's wife. Maybe it was better this way. It wasn't that strange to Cindy that her new family would be living so close at hand. Her oldest brother Terry, who had married the year before, lived in the house right next door to Gladys and R.G. She would be getting her own house, eventually. Until then, she would get to know the family. She would learn to speak Arabic. She would be patient.

In other ways, Cindy was unprepared for what life would be like in the Middle East; there were customs she didn't understand. She had not thought to ask many questions – she didn't know what to ask. People had told her that she would have to cover herself up, and that Mohammed could have other wives. Cindy couldn't believe that Mohammed would force her to cover, or do anything else she didn't want to do. She certainly couldn't imagine him wanting another wife. He was devoted to her, she knew it. She had not thought about the challenges she might face – it seemed that she and Mohammed had more in common than their differences. Faith in God, no premarital sex, and no alcohol. Neither had thought much about their differences, obvious as they were. They were young and in love. Cindy had married Mohammed on faith. In those first weeks, in a foreign land, a strange world, with no command of the language, she would learn to adjust. Whatever came her way, she was determined to deal with it.

Suddenly she was overcome with thirst. The mid-July sun was hammering the pavement under them, the roof of the car. The air conditioning was almost useless. She'd seen a bottle of water rolling around and, finding it, uncapped it to take a drink.

"Stop!" Mohammed cried. "What are you doing? You cannot drink water in public! Put it down!"

"What?"

"It is Ramadan!" he was panic-stricken. "It is against the law! You can be arrested and go to jail! *Put it down!"*

"You mean people can't drink water? Even me? But I'm not Muslim –" she'd been allowed to eat breakfast that morning –

"Look, Honey. Even you cannot drink in public. It is out of respect for others who fast," he said.

Mohammed had told her that Muslim people fast during the holy month of Ramadan, but she didn't know it was so strict. During the day, Muslims did not allow even a single drop of water pass through their lips. During the day, while the sun was up, smoking, gum chewing, and sex were also forbidden. Why had Mohammed not warned her of this? He had, she now began to realize, told her very little about what her new life would be like.

"Yes! Yes, I did tell you." he insisted. "You do not listen. You only hear what you want to hear. Not what you don't want to hear." Cindy laughed. It was true. She could readily block out, ignore, or brush off what she didn't want to know. She'd been too busy planning the wedding to think about anything else. Mohammed had probably told her things and she just hadn't paid attention, or not understood. Theirs was a love with a language barrier. But it didn't matter, she would learn fast enough, God willing. *Inshallah.*

The sun was sinking low in the sky. "Time to go home," Mohammed said, as Cindy felt a wave of love, mixed with exhaustion, wash over her. "Tomorrow I go back to the base, and you will be with the ladies. But Abdulrahman will be there to help you. He will translate."

Chapter 6: Married to Mohammed

1982

When Cindy and Mohammed married, the Middle East was facing a rising tide of instability. The Iranian revolution overthrown Mohammed Reza Shah Pahlavi, known as the Shah of Iran, in 1979, replacing his secular government with the Ayatollah Khomeini who established a hardline Islamist Shia government. As Cindy arrived in the UAE, Iran and Iraq were in the second year of what would become a brutal eight-year war initiated by Iraqi leader Saddam Hussein. Neither side would win a decisive victory, but the war would result in millions of casualties and lost lives, and hundreds of billions of dollars in damage. Arriving as a young, naïve bride, the turbulence was too complicated for Cindy to understand, but married to Mohammed, she would learn. There were two things at the heart of it: oil and religion.

As the UAE was building its infrastructure, its education system, its population and its cultural identity, it was also building its defense capabilities. Mohammed was in the Army, and he lived and worked in the large military complex called Zayed Military City, in Abu Dhabi. That first Saturday morning, he was gone.

Mohammed's house was only a few years old, but small. In the UAE, the effects of oil money were felt first in the cities, enjoyed by the ruling families and those with *wasta,* or influence. It would eventually filter out to the general population, to those outside of the large and shining urban centers of Abu Dhabi and Dubai, and the historic oasis at Al Ain. But for now, most of the resources, human if not financial, were occupied in just trying to set up a functioning government under constantly changing circumstances.

The government's program of awarding plots of land to Emirati nationals, and providing zero-interest construction financing, meant that Khorfakkan now had modern, if modest, homes. Mohammed's house had a small living room, or *majlis,* with a bathroom at one end and at the other a hall leading to the two bedrooms. There was another room which served as the kitchen and a tiny, windowless room, no bigger than a closet, in which the houseboy lived. Mohammed and Cindy occupied one of the bedrooms and Abdulrahman, his wife, and their two young daughters occupied the other. Abduls' wife Maryam was expecting their third child. Their new house was nearby, still under construction, and the family would be moving there soon, *inshallah*. Until then they were living under Mohammed's roof, as was the other brother, Hassan Ali, who slept in the living room. A group of Pakistanis, friends of the family, worked in the garage, doing who knows what, and they slept in the living room as well. It was there, in that crowded house, that Cindy began her life as a newlywed.

Those first days, Cindy absorbed her first real Arab words, the language that she would use in everyday conversation, as she learned about Arab food. The Islam required that during the holy month of Ramadan, the days be spent in fasting, prayer, sacrifice, and generosity toward the less fortunate. But Ramadan was also a time of celebration and delicious food. After sundown, they ate a special meal called *iftar*. Sometimes people stayed up far into the night eating, talking, and celebrating. Then, just before the sun rose, they prayed, and ate a meal called *suhoor* which would have to last them all day until they broke the fast again at sundown. This staying up at night was normal for them, and it was summer, so there was no school for the children. Sleeping was a daytime activity, something to do when it was too hot to do anything else. Sometimes people didn't get up until 4:00 p.m. Workdays were shorter during Ramadan, starting later and ending earlier.

Despite fasting all day, people didn't hurry to eat a large meal as soon as the sun set. Instead, they let their stomachs slowly adjust to food after the daylong fast. Just after sunset, when they heard the *muzzein* call an end to the fasting, they drank a glass of water and ate three dates – only three – because the Prophet had always eaten an odd number of dates. Then they went to the mosque for evening prayer – well, the men went to their mosque while most of the women, although they had their own separate mosque, stayed and prayed at home so that they could care for the children. After prayer was over, a meal was served. The wealthiest families erected tents where they served their large extended families and other members of the community, with leftovers distributed to those less fortunate. The mosque also provided a meal which was enjoyed by families of more modest means, workers, and the poor. Some nights Mohammed's family celebrated *iftar* at the mosque, some nights they ate a simple meal at home, and on Friday, they met and celebrated *iftar* at an auntie's house. No one, no matter how poor, went hungry during Ramadan.

Cindy couldn't believe the amount of food that was served at *iftar* but, to her surprise, she liked at least some of it. The meal usually started with a glutinous, oatmeal-colored dish called *harees,* made with wheat berries that were soaked for several hours, then simmered with meat – perhaps lamb or goat – and spiced with cinnamon. It was served with a generous swirl of melted butter on top. Everyone seemed to love it, gulping it down and reaching for seconds.

After the *harees* came a dish called *thareed*: several layers of crispy flatbread layered with a meat stew. The meat was deliciously fragrant with cardamom, coriander, black lemon, and chili. Cindy found the dish filling and satisfying, but there was something about the meat, which was always hacked into unidentifiable pieces with bone, sinew, and fat attached, that didn't agree with her. From then on, whenever she was served a dish with meat, she left the meat on the plate. This worked out well because if she had finished all the food, someone would immediately heap more onto her plate. That was the Arab way, Mohammed told her – no guest could have an empty plate. It was a sign that they hadn't been served enough.

She loved the *samboosas.* They were like the Indian *samosas* that they'd had on their first date, but with a local flavor, an Emirati spice called *bezar.* It was a blend of cumin, coriander, nutmeg, cloves, turmeric, and something else she couldn't identify. She looked for the vegetable ones, avoiding the meat. And there was always a rice dish, *machboos,* long-grain white rice mixed with meat, chicken, or shrimp, and vegetables. There were many different kinds, but again, it was the combination of spices that made it special. She could eat the delicious rice with the vegetables, and chicken if it was available, although the Emiratis always seemed to prefer meat.

Emirati food had many influences – Lebanese, Indian, and Egyptian among them – but it had developed its own character. It was unique. It was not as spicy as the Indian food that she and Mohammed had discovered each other over, yet Emirati cooks used a blend of ingredients that made their dishes far from bland. Saffron, cardamom, chili, coriander, cinnamon, nutmeg, dried lemon, turmeric – some day she would learn them all.

There was always an array of delicious desserts. The sweet, flaky phyllo *baklava* pastries appeared in so many shapes – diamonds, fingers, triangles – and were filled or topped with mixed ground pistachios and walnuts. There was a rice pudding called *firni* with saffron and nuts, and tubs of sticky-sweet gelatinous *halwa*. Cindy's favorite was *luqaimat* – which she thought of as donut holes, or maybe Arabic hush puppies. Flour and yeast, with a bit of mashed potato for crunchiness, were mixed and spiced with saffron and cardamom, left to rise, then formed into balls, deep fried, and drizzled with date syrup or honey.

It was the *Umm Ali* that everyone prized. Once Cindy tasted it, she knew why. It was bread pudding, but instead of using plain bread it was made with rich pastry dough, cooked in a sweet cream sauce thick with dried fruit – raisins, currants, apricots, and prunes, and dusted with ground toasted pistachios, hazelnuts, and walnuts, and a bit of shredded coconut. This sublime dessert was on the table at every celebration. It was heaven in a bowl.

Mohammed hadn't told Cindy much about the Muslim religion or its customs, but her own Independent Baptist upbringing in North Carolina had prepared her well. As she listened to the conversations around her, she began to hear the same syllables over and over – *allah*.

"Bismallah." When they were going somewhere in the car. *"Bismallah."* Murmured as they sat down to eat. *"Bismallah."* When they went for a walk.

"It means, 'In the name of Allah,'" Mohammed's brother Abdulrahman told her when she asked about it. It was like a prayer before meals, but they said it as a prayer before *everything*.

"Just as *inshallah* means 'If Allah wills.' Whenever we want to say that something could happen or we might do it. And *subhanalla* means 'Glory to Allah,' we say it when something is amazing, and *mashallah* means 'As Allah wishes,' when we are amazed for something that is very good."

"What about *alhamdulillah?*" Cindy asked. "I hear that all the time."

"That is 'Praise God,'" Abdul replied. "We say that when we are satisfied, as after a meal. When someone asks how we are they say, '*Kayfa halak?*' and we say '*Ana bikhayr alhamdulillah.*' 'I am fine, praise Allah.'"

Praise God. Praise the Lord. The very same expression that I've been hearing and saying all my life. Alhamdulillah. She began to feel that she could break this mysterious code that was Arabic.

That first week was long, and the one-day weekends far too short. Cindy was desperate to spend more time with Mohammed. At the end of their second weekend together in Khorfakkan, Mohammed arranged for one of the Pakistanis, his good friend Shaukat, to drive him to the base so that Cindy could come along for the ride. After dropping Mohammed off, they would return home to Khorfakkan. It meant an entire day of driving across the rugged, remote mountains, first to Dubai, and then across the empty coastal desert to the base just outside Abu Dhabi. And then back again. Between cities, there was nothing. Cindy didn't care that she would be spending all day driving; she just wanted more time with Mohammed. It was a chance to sit beside him.

Cindy liked Shaukat. He was her favorite of the Pakistani men who lived in Mohammed's house, working during the day, and sleeping in the crowded living room at night. She enjoyed his easygoing company and appreciated his desire to learn a bit of English by speaking with her. She and Shaukat wouldn't be driving back alone, though; Zamzam was coming along as well.

Nothing escaped Zamzam's watchful eye and sharp ear, and whenever she caught wind of the fact that someone was going somewhere, she demanded to go, too. Besides, some people might think it wasn't acceptable for Cindy to be driving alone with Shaukat, a man who was not her husband, brother, or father. If there were two ladies, then it would not look so bad. Cindy didn't mind Zamzam's company; she was just desperately happy for the chance to be near Mohammed for a bit longer.

After they'd been on the road for several hours, Cindy realized, to her dismay, that her period was starting. She wasn't expecting this, and wasn't prepared. She was especially worried because she was wearing her good light pink pants, not her usual blue jeans. They were in the bleakly empty desert between Dubai and Abu Dhabi, where there were no filling stations, no rest stops, no convenience stores. Nothing. She confided her problem to Mohammed in a whisper, even though neither Shaukat nor Zamzam would understand what she was saying to him. It wasn't that bad yet, she said; they would be turning around at the base, and she could wait until they made it back to Dubai. Surely then there would be a store they could stop at. Mohammed spoke a few words to Zamzam, telling her to help Cindy on the way back.

After dropping Mohammed at the dusty base near Al Bateen Airport on the island of Abu Dhabi, they headed back toward Dubai and the real problems began. They had a flat tire. With no spare – Emiratis never carried spares – and nothing along the road until Dubai, there was no choice but to flag down a passing vehicle and catch a ride. Fortunately, all the traffic whizzing by on this lonely road was going to Dubai, and they easily caught a ride which took them all the way, where they went to the home of a Pakistani family that Shaukat knew. The woman there was kind, but nobody spoke English. She went into the bathroom. There was the usual cleansing hose, which had multiple uses including cleaning oneself after toileting and washing before prayer. There was no toilet paper, no box of tissues. These people didn't use these things. They used water and, if needed, their left hand, to cleanse themselves.

Cindy cleaned up the best she could, and returned to the living room, where the wife encouraged her to sleep on the couch. But Cindy couldn't go to sleep. Not only was she worried about soiling the couch, but it was 2 a.m., and she had been wearing her contact lenses all day. She needed to take them out to go to sleep. But those supplies, the solution and the case, were back home in her room – along with the pads that she desperately wished she had. She couldn't explain all this to the woman, who wondered why in the world Cindy was sitting awake, instead of closing her eyes and resting.

For some reason, Zamzam never spoke to the Pakistani woman about Cindy's period, and Cindy had no delicate way to tell her about it herself. Too young, shy, and modest, she waited for Shaukat's return with the repaired tire, and they would be on their way back to Khorfakkan. She could manage for now, and the drive from Dubai to Fujairah, where she could use a bathroom, was only a couple of hours.

Finally, at dawn, Shaukat returned and they were on the road again. Then – unbelievably – another flat tire! By now, Cindy was ready to laugh. Who would even believe this story? Again, they were in the middle of nowhere, and again there was nothing to do but flag someone down. This time, they went to the house of an Emirati family friend in Fujairah who Zamzam knew, and whom Cindy already had met, where the father and his young daughter knew some English.

Then, inexplicably, Zamzam suddenly remembered her instructions from Mohammed. Cindy heard her say something to the daughter, and caught a word that she recognized: *Kotex.* Kotex! That was the Arab word for sanitary pad. If only she had known, she could have asked the Pakistani woman at the house in Dubai.

Oh, my God. Of course, that makes so much sense. Products were known by their brand names. If she went to the store and looked around, she would know what to ask for next time something like this happened. She'd come all this way, they were almost home, so close it didn't matter much anymore. Nevertheless, it was a relief to finally stop worrying.

Years later, she met the father again. He looked at her quizzically. "I don't know if you remember me –" he began. Cindy looked at the man and thought of her young, newlywed self in the pale pink pants, struggling for two days on the road with Zamzam. She recalled the shock of hearing a familiar word – *Kotex* – and her frustration at having been too shy to speak out, to try to communicate. How absurd it all seemed now. But she smiled, recalling the powerful lesson she'd learned that day.

"Oh yes, I remember you," Cindy told Mr. Kotex. "I'll never forget you." He would never know why.

Chapter 7: Zamzam

"I am no good at English," Hassan Ali laughed. During those first few weeks, Mohammed's younger brother accompanied Cindy whenever she took a walk around the neighborhood or into town. Eager to practice, he would try to speak English with her, joking about his lack of skills.

Cindy was learning Arabic, and she had the same problems that Hassan had with English. Sometimes it was difficult to distinguish words that sounded similar, like egg, house, and white – they all sounded like *"bait"* to her ear. And there were other problems – Arabic verbs were all in the present, and Cindy was used to speaking in past and future tenses. While Hassan was always using the present tense incorrectly, Cindy was trying to figure out how to frame a question about the past, or the future, in Arabic.

But some words sounded much the same – *limun* was a familiar word for citrus, and she also recognized the Arab pronunciation for *alcohol*, which was forbidden in the Muslim religion just as it was in her own. When they had to pay a fee, it was a *tariff*, the word for *camel* was the same, and its feed was *alfalfa*. And a *million* was a million. *Dirhams* were the Emirati currency.

Hassan Ali, the youngest child and a boy, was spoiled and unbelievably immature, a trait which he had inherited from his mother, and she had cultivated. Zamzam and Hassan quarreled endlessly. Hassan wanted to get married. No! Zamzam refused to hear of it. Why did her son want to get married? He knew nothing! He was just a boy! And yet, when it served some purpose, when she needed something to brag about, Zamzam would hold her son up as a man.

"*Mashallah,* my son is here to take me home," she would say when he arrived at the end of a day of visiting. "He is the only one who does things for me. All the others, they do nothing." Then, on the way home, she would berate him for walking too fast, she couldn't keep up, typical man. Or they were going too slow – why was he dawdling like a child? No wonder Hassan was such a boy, Cindy thought. He was told he was a man, and then he was told that he wasn't – when nothing had changed.

Still, Cindy had to agree with Zamzam when it came to Hassan's immaturity. She liked Hassan, but sometimes he acted so childish. He was always joking about silly things, and it seemed like he didn't know anything about life. Certainly, nothing about women. One weekend about a month after she arrived, Cindy was suffering from menstrual cramps and doubled over with pain. Mohammed comforted her while Zamzam and Hassan watched with curiosity.

"What is wrong with her?" Zamzam asked, although she surely could have guessed.

"She has her period," Mohammed answered.

"Congratulations!" Hassan exclaimed. "I hope it's a boy!"

He thinks I'm having a baby? Cindy thought. *Doesn't he know anything?* Everyone assumed that Cindy would become pregnant immediately after the wedding, but she and Mohammed had decided to wait. Zamzam couldn't understand why she was having a period, why wasn't she pregnant yet? What was wrong with her? But Hassan Ali, didn't he know that she couldn't possibly be having a baby yet? They had only been married for six weeks.

Cindy didn't need Hassan to escort her around town for long. In just a few weeks she got her UAE driver's license. It didn't require much – just a letter of permission from her husband. A letter of permission! But it was ok, Cindy decided. That was just the way things were done there. Anything she wanted, Mohammed wanted her to have. Whereas some husbands tried to control their wives, his only wish was to make things easier for her. To make her happy. He even bought her a nice little BMW sedan, and then she was the driver while Hassan rode.

It was 1982, and Cindy was the second woman in Khorfakkan to drive. Around town, going places, doing errands, she found that when she introduced herself, people already knew who she was. *"Assalamu alaikam,"* they said. She now recognized the greeting that meant, "Hello, peace be upon you." And using her new Arabic, filling in with gestures, they could communicate. Yes, yes, you are Mohammed Ali's wife, the American. The white lady from *Amereeeka*. She was a local celebrity.

Despite being surrounded by people most of the time, Cindy was desperately lonely for Mohammed when he was gone during the week. It was too hot to go outside during the daylight hours, people were fasting, and they slept most of the day, while Cindy crept into the kitchen for a snack or some iced tea, carrying it to her room to eat in private. She had brought only two books with her, and one was the Bible. She would have brought more if she'd realized that there was virtually nothing in English to be found, anywhere. Within a month, she would know *Gone with the Wind* almost by heart.

When she wasn't in her room, Cindy spent her time visiting with the countless relatives that lived in the neighborhood. Mohammed's three older children, the boys Jassim, Ali, and Ahmed, were living with their grandparents, Zamzam and Ali Mubarak. Cindy often went over there, trying to get to know them although, being boys, they were not particularly interested and Zamzam was no help when it came to warming the boys up to Cindy.

Mohammed's ex-wife, Aisha, lived nearby with their daughter Maryam. In a divorce, the children stay with the father, not the mother, unless they are younger than five years old and therefore allowed to stay with the mother. Aisha was still part of the family, and she was sometimes present when Cindy went visiting at the house of an auntie or cousin. Anyone who was related was an uncle or auntie if they were older, and a cousin if they were about the same age. It didn't matter if they were a first, second, or third cousin – or even more tangentially related; nobody kept track. First cousins often married, the brothers of one family married the sisters in another. If they were to construct a family tree, which they didn't bother to do, it would be more a web than a tree. But they didn't need it, because they all had a family name. It was the name of their tribe. Mohammed's name was Al Hammadi, but that would never become Cindy's name, because women always kept their own tribal name, even after marriage. She would always be Cindy Davis.

One of Cindy's brothers had asked her why she wouldn't take Mohammed's last name, as American women did. "I married him," she replied. "He didn't adopt me."

Despite Zamzam's coolness, the other ladies took Cindy under their wing, especially Zamzam's sister, Auntie Fatima, who had greeted her so kindly that first night. What Zamzam lacked in warmth, Fatima made up for twofold. Every day, Cindy walked over to her house to use the telephone to call Mohammed at the base. She told him what she was doing, and he talked about life on the base, told her a funny story to make her laugh, and they made plans for Friday, *inshallah*. The rest of her day was spent reading alone and visiting with the ladies who came to visit, unless she went to their house first.

It was the last week of July, and everyone was preparing for Eid al-Fitr, a three-day religious holiday marking the end of Ramadan and the breaking of the month-long fast. Everyone was waiting in anticipation for the announcement of when it would begin. The exact day could only be set after it was determined whether the moon could be sighted just after sunset when the lunar month ended. Unlike the solar Gregorian calendar that Cindy was used to, the Muslim calendar was a lunar calendar consisting of 12 months of 29 days each, and 354 or 355 days in a year. The holy month of Ramadan and all religious holidays revolved around the solar year according to this lunar calendar. Cindy had wondered, when she first arrived and found that it was Ramadan and everyone was fasting, why they would choose midsummer, the time of the most intense heat and the longest days, to be forbidden to drink even a drop of water. Wasn't that unhealthy, even dangerous? It would change, she now realized. With fewer days in the Muslim calendar, it would come a bit sooner each year. Quickly calculating in her head, she determined that the next time Ramadan would occur in July again as it did this year would be 2012. She and Mohammed would have just celebrated their 30th anniversary, *inshallah*.

Fatima's daughters, Fatima, Maryam, and Aisha, and the other young cousins near Cindy's age, liked to dress up, and Eid al-Fitr, in addition to being a time of prayer, was a time of celebration and gift-giving. Women and young girls dressed in all their finery, and Fatima's daughters brought out armloads of colorful, silky dresses, ornately beaded head scarves and headdresses, jewelry, and makeup. Cindy, with her pale skin and soft auburn hair, was their new plaything. Clucking around her, speaking words she was beginning to understand, they dressed her in a dazzling costume, lining her eyes with black kohl so that she looked like Cleopatra.

"'Ant jamila!" You are beautiful! They gathered around her, giggling and chattering, as the oldest cousin Fatima snapped pictures with a Polaroid camera. Cindy felt like a princess.

The dressing-up was only a game; when it was time to celebrate with the family, Cindy had a new dress, custom-made by the tailor. She had chosen the fabric, a satiny polyester in a beautiful emerald green that set off her pale, luminous complexion and brought out the fiery highlights in her hair. Shimmering gold-threaded trim framed the neckline and sleeves and embroidery decorated the fitted bodice, which showed off her tiny waist and curves. The skirt reached to the floor, and the sleeves went to her wrists, so that she would be properly covered. She was quite proud of this first party dress.

When Zamzam saw Cindy, she did not look pleased. *"Wahu housedress!"* she said. *"Limadha housedress!"* The word, spoken in Arabic, sounded like "haeesddess," but by now Cindy knew enough Arabic to realize what Zamzam had said. It was a housedress. Why was she wearing a housedress? Cindy was shocked. A housedress was a plain dress, not suitable for Eid.

"Do you think this looks like a housedress?" she asked her sister-in-law Maryam, Abdulrahman's wife.

"Laa," Maryam shook her head. "No, it is ok. It is a pretty dress. Do not listen to Zamzam, she is never happy. She likes to complain about everyone. Do not change it."

She doesn't like the dress? She doesn't like me.

Cindy loved the dress, and she wasn't going to change out of it to satisfy Zamzam, who would probably only find something to criticize again. *Too bad. It's her problem. If she doesn't like it she can just look the other way.* Zamzam's disapproval only made Cindy like the dress more. From then on, she decided, she would wear it as often as she could.

Zamzam wasn't finished criticizing. As they sat in the ladies' *majlis,* Zamzam waved a hand in Cindy's direction and announced, for all to hear, *"Waqalat 'annaha tartadi 'ahmar alshshifah!"* Cindy knew she was being accused of something, but those last two words were unfamiliar.

"She says you wear lipstick," a cousin told her. Wearing lipstick in public was *haram* – bad.

"Laa-laa!" Cindy protested. She was *not* wearing lipstick. This was the natural color of her lips. No one ever believed it.

"La yuhimm," the cousin replied, waving her own hand back in Zamzam's direction. "Doesn't matter. She just says these things."

A young cousin pointed to Cindy and asked who had put on her eyeliner.

"I did it myself." Too shy to answer in Arabic, Cindy replied in English, patting her chest to show her meaning. She took pride in her steady hand applying the kohl so that she looked just like the others.

"La 'amrika tastatie 'an tafeal dhalik," The cousin said. No American can do that. *"La yumkin 'illa 'an alearab tafeal dhalik."* Only Arabs can do it. Understanding the words but unable to reply, Cindy just shook her head slightly, and the conversation moved on. The cousin's eyes remained on Cindy for a few moments longer before she turned away.

After that, whenever Cindy tried to apply eye liner, her hand shook. It was strange, because she'd never had a tremor before. And it only happened when she was trying to apply eyeliner.

Her sister-in-law Maryam observed her struggle and remarked, "Someone has put the eye on you." The jealous cousin had cursed Cindy with the evil eye. She would never be able to put eyeliner on properly again. Eventually, she gave up.

Cindy was learning enough Arabic to understand most of what was said in daily conversation, but she was still too shy to speak it, for fear she would make some awful blunder. Meanwhile Zamzam always had some criticism to which Cindy had no ready reply. She usually addressed her complaints to others but in front of Cindy, as if she weren't there. Why didn't she eat more? Didn't she like the food? Was it no good? If she was a local lady, she would eat. Mohammed should have a wife who is a local.

I tried to eat the meat in the rice dish. It makes my stomach sick.

Why did she water the tree? She kills it with water!

I thought it needed watering – it's so hot.

Why didn't she water the tree? She kills it with thirst!

I thought she didn't want me watering it.

Why did she wear that? Where did she go? Why didn't she take Zamzam?

If I have to take you everywhere, I'll NEVER go out anywhere!

Zamzam took to calling Mohammed at the base, demanding, "Do you know what that wife of yours did today?" Zamzam the informant was calling Mohammed to tattle on Cindy. She was trying to drive a wedge between them. *Well, I'll fix that,* Cindy thought. *I can do her one better.*

Mohammed got a telephone installed in the house, so that Cindy wouldn't have to go to Auntie Fatima's house any longer. Now, each morning, she could call Mohammed before Zamzam had a chance. If she made plans or did something unexpected, she called to tell him. It became their little joke but, more than that, it cemented their bond. Somehow, if she spoke with him a couple of times a day or more, if she could call him any time, about anything, he didn't seem so far away, and the days went by faster.

While Cindy was learning Arabic, she was also picking up some proper English. Colleen was from London, and she was Cindy's only English speaking friend that first year. Colleen lived close enough that they could walk to each other's house and they relied on each other's company, becoming close friends. Cindy enjoyed the chance to speak English and talk about their shared experience as foreign wives.

One day, they decided to go up into the mountains for a picnic at the Wadi Wurayah waterfall. Although Cindy had her license and her own car by then, the BMW was only safe for driving in town, not up into the rugged Hajar mountains, which required a four-wheel drive. She asked Shaukat the Pakistani who lived in the house to drive them. Shaukat was a good friend, trustworthy, and Cindy saw nothing wrong with it. Most Arab ladies had drivers.

The day was lovely, breezy and warm. They left the turquoise blue of the Indian Ocean below, and climbed into the mountains. Cindy, who was never much of a beach person, had always loved her family's trips into the rolling green highlands of North Carolina. These mountains were different, rockier, with very few trees. But compared to most of the UAE, which was desert, they were beautiful, and they reminded her of home.

Shaukat drove up a dirt road alongside a *wadi*. As they ascended, the hardscrabble landscape was transformed into a lush wetland. Reaching the waterfall, they gazed below to where the flow split, and split again, forming several, and then hundreds, of small streams whose banks were lined with reeds, grasses, and small shrubs. Dragonflies hovered nearby, glittering and silent.

Shaukat wandered off to rest and relax at a respectful distance while Cindy and Colleen laid out their picnic of pita bread, hummus, olives, cheese balls, and fresh fruit. Over lunch, Cindy confided to Colleen about Zamzam. "She drives me kind of crazy. She criticizes everything I do, and everything I buy. At the same time, she can't stand it when I get something that she doesn't have. I bought a handbag last week, and she said it looked ugly. This week, I see she has the same bag. Exactly the same! She criticizes, but then she can't stand it when I have something she doesn't have. She has to have it, too."

Colleen smiled in empathy, but when she talked about her adjustment to life as an Arab wife, her problems seemed bigger. She was having trouble getting along with her husband. They had lived together in England while Ahmed was in school, and they had a child. It was an exciting, modern love affair, at least while they were still in England. But then, Ahmed had been offered a job in his own country and before they could move to the UAE they needed to marry. Living together without marriage was forbidden.

"He wants me to cover all the time," Colleen said. "I don't want to. He wants me to pray, to read the Quran. He expects me to become a Muslim. I have my own religion and I thought he understood and accepted that. I think his family is pressuring him about it. Why don't they just leave us alone?" Colleen loved Ahmed, but she felt the weight of the family's judgement upon her.

And there was another, bigger problem. In the UAE, their child would not be recognized as Ahmed's son, because he was born out of wedlock. He was not of the marriage. So, they had made a photocopy of their marriage certificate, changed the date to the year before the baby was born, and recopied it. The government officials were none the wiser, but Ahmed's family surely knew, and those that didn't know probably suspected. It had seemed very romantic and exciting then, but now, the reality of her situation was hitting Colleen. She was British. She came from a culture of neighborhood pubs, not neighborhood mosques. And who was this man she was married to, who dressed in a *kandura* and waved her off into a different room to socialize with only women, with whom Colleen had nothing in common? He was not the Arab prince that she had once seen him as. And, now that they were back in the UAE and living under Sharia law, how did he feel about their deception? What did his family say? She didn't know; it was never spoken of between them. Ahmed refused to discuss it, even when they were alone. It was as if he thought someone was listening.

"It is nice enough here, I won't deny that'" Colleen admitted. "The weather is brilliant. But the shops are appalling." For the Londoner, the little Arab outpost on the coast of the Indian Ocean was becoming less exotic and more confining each day. To lighten the mood, Cindy told Colleen a shopping story.

"I went into a store for milk. I used the Arab word, *halib*. He takes me to this aisle where they have all this stuff in cans and boxes, all at room temperature. 'No,' I said, 'I don't want that. I want milk.' He couldn't figure out what I meant. I tried to explain that the milk I wanted was cold. I kept saying '*bard,*' for 'cold.' Finally, he said, 'Ah, *taazaj!*

Fresh milk! We don't have that.' I don't think there's any place in town that sells real milk." Cindy didn't like the flavor of the long-life milk, which was processed at a high temperature to give it a long shelf life in the heat. It had a flat, cooked flavor. But there was no choice, and what could you do? Just laugh. Eventually, there would be stores that carried fresh milk, but that was still in the future.

That afternoon, when Cindy got home from the picnic, Zamzam was at the house, seething, stomping around, banging and slamming anything she could put her hands on. Cindy phoned Mohammed.

"Today my mother call me," he said, and Cindy could hear the smile in his voice. "She say, 'Do you know what that crazy wife of yours does now?' I say, 'Yes. She is at the *wadi* with her friend.' My mother say, 'You know about this?' *Hamdallah,* I did know because you call me first."

"Why is she so upset about it?" Cindy wondered aloud.

"The *djinn* live in the mountains," Mohammed said. "She thinks you anger them, bring bad to our house."

"What is *djinn?*" Cindy asked. "You need to tell me about this."

Mohammed explained. A *djinni* was a supernatural being, able to take many forms. They were usually invisible, but they had the ability to shape-shift into any insect, animal, or human form. *Djinn* appeared throughout the Quran as invisible creatures made of smokeless fire, one of the three kinds of beings created by God – the others being humans, who were made of clay, and angels, made of light. Mohammed said that the *djinn* preferred unpopulated places to cities, and therefore the mountains, the sea, and the air around Khorfakkan and neighboring Oman were full of them. *Djinn* could be good, evil, or neutral. They were invisible, but they had weight – if one sat on you, you would feel its weight upon you. And it could feel your weight, as well. If you accidentally sat or stepped on a *djinni,* watch out. You were probably in for some trouble. Evil *djinn* were *shaytan,* devils, and Satan, a *djinni* who was cast out of Paradise, was their leader.

"They're *haints!*" Cindy said. "Back home in North Carolina, there's all kinds of stories about ghosts, hauntings, and the Devil." She remembered of some of the stories. There was the Devil's Stompin' Ground, about an hour and a half drive east of Mocksville. It was a place where nothing would grow. People said it was because the Devil paced there every night, thinking of ways to poison people's souls and bring them to damnation. Those who tried to spend the night there went insane. And there were all kinds of haunted houses, including the Governor's Mansion, which was said to be haunted by a former governor, upset because his specially made oversized bed had been moved out of his bedroom. There was a haunted house in nearby Winston-Salem, just a half hour away from Mocksville. A shoemaker in a red hat, who was buried alive when they were digging the foundation, was heard banging a hammer, and seen scurrying around in his red hat for years until a minister was called in to drive him away.

And then there was the Wampus Cat. There were so many stories about the Cattywampus, as some people called it, they were too many to count. The cat was said to be a Cherokee woman who had spied on her husband and his hunting party as they prepared for their hunt, causing her to be changed into a mixture of human and cougar. She was doomed to roam the mountains alone at night, stealing farm animals, breaking things, and just generally upsetting people's apple cart. When something was messed up, or askew, people said it was 'cattywampus.'

"But I don't believe all these stories," she said to Mohammed. "I think people hear something, or see something, and their imagination gets the best of them. And in North Carolina, people just love to tell the stories. Those haunted houses make good tourist attractions, too. Do you really believe in *djinn?"*

"Yes, it is true," Mohammed said. "But don't worry. If something happens, it happens. You deal with it, and then it is over, *inshallah.* It won't be too bad. *Inshallah."*

Cindy suspected that her trip to the mountains wouldn't have been such an outrage if Zamzam had been invited along, even though she couldn't imagine that woman climbing around and sitting on the rocks, as she and Colleen had. But you never knew. After all, Zamzam had been born among the rocks, and had borne her children the same way, in a cave. Thank God, she'd called Mohammed. Zamzam could not make trouble between them. And now, she knew about the *djinn*. No wonder they loved movies like *The Amityville Horror*.

After that day, Cindy made doubly sure she called Mohammed first if she went out and did something. "I'm going to the tailor with Colleen, and afterward we're going to walk along the Corniche." Or, "We're going shopping, and then lunch, and then to the beauty salon." Or, "I'm going out for some new linens for the house." Then, she would pick up her handbag and the car keys and drive off, leaving Zamzam, who always seemed to be watching from her house, to scheme and vent. It didn't matter what it was, or how innocent. Zamzam would inevitably call her son and demand, "Do you know what that wife of yours is doing?" And Mohammed could truthfully answer, "Yes." Thus, the wind was taken out of Zamzam's sails. But more importantly, Cindy and Mohammed developed a pattern of communication during the long weekdays while they were apart. In this way, rather than Zamzam driving a wedge between them, she made them stronger.

Cindy was settling into her new life in this new country, with Mohammed and his family. Yes, it was boring during the week and sometimes it seemed that all she did was read. And she craved anything and everything American. There was still only the one television station, which broadcast from Abu Dhabi. The American soap operas and prime time dramas and comedies that they did show were already old. Oh, how she craved news about home. What she wouldn't give for an American newspaper. But she didn't want to be a complainer. People like her and Colleen, who came from Western countries, were spoiled. What did they expect when they moved here? That everything would be the same? That they could still have all the comforts of home?

That September, Abdulrahman's house was finally finished and ready for move-in, greatly easing the crowded living arrangement. Shaukat and the other two Pakistani men went back to Pakistan, Hassan moved into Zamzam and Ali Mubarak's house, and the houseboy was sent away. After they all moved out, Mohammed's two younger sons, Ali and Ahmed, and his daughter Maryam moved into the house with Cindy, while the eldest son Jassim stayed in Zamzam's house to help his grandmother. For a couple of months, Cindy and Mohammed enjoyed more space and privacy, and the children were good company for Cindy during the week. She was enjoying a kind of domestic bliss that she hadn't known before. Then Mohammed received a training assignment in Saudi Arabia. He would be gone for several weeks.

The day that he left, the door opened and in walked Zamzam and Ali, along with Mohammed's brother Hassan, his son Jassim, and Zamzam's housemaid. They had all come to live with Cindy and the other children in Mohammed's absence. Nobody had warned her, and nobody had asked her opinion, let alone her permission. Or Mohammed's, for that matter. They just arrived, unannounced, and moved in as if they owned the place. Because in their minds, they did. It was Mohammed's house; thus, it was also theirs and they would do as they saw fit. Cindy was powerless to stop them. When she spoke with Mohammed on the phone, she complained vehemently.

"Why do they all have to move in here?" she asked, her voice rising and the words tumbling over themselves. "They already have a house! I don't want them here! I don't need them here. I like just living with the kids."

But Mohammed begged her to accommodate them. "It's ok, just until I come back," he promised. "Honey, Please. Just let it go. For my sake." And that was Mohammed. His job was to keep the family at peace. He was caught between his American wife, who he wanted to keep happy, and his Arab family, who he must keep happy. Cindy knew that everything that Mohammed was doing, he did out of love and duty. His duty to his family did not diminish the love he had for her. Yes, he wanted her to be happy and she would be happier with her own house. But she wanted him to be happy, and that meant helping him to keep his family happy. This wouldn't last forever. Eventually they would move to Abu Dhabi, *inshallah.* The family would never follow them there.

When Mohammed came home from Saudi Arabia, they made up for the time they spent apart. Behind their closed door, Cindy and Mohammed grew closer, delighting in their shared stories, repeating funny anecdotes about crazy Zamzam or silly Hassan even though they'd already been shared over the phone. And they enjoyed their long-awaited intimacy. He was her protector, her validator, her rock. She knew that no matter what, he would accept her, come to her defense, and support her in whatever way she needed him.

But if it felt like they were still always being watched that was because – well – they were. Hassan had – incredibly – gotten married, and he and his wife moved into Ali Mubarak and Zamzam's house. But Zamzam, who was apparently less willing to put up with the presence of Hassan's new Indian wife than with Cindy, remained in Mohammed's house.

Soon there was another reason why Zamzam wouldn't move out of their house. Ali Mubarak had another wife. This was most Arab wives' greatest fear, and the ultimate insult. Zamzam, who was always complaining bitterly of being wronged, now had something to be justly enraged over. Ali Mubarak had married a local widow, and her house was just across the street from his. The banging and slamming was constant, as Zamzam spewed her anger and frustration. Again, Cindy objected and again, Mohammed begged for her patience.

"Please, Honey. We will move to Abu Dhabi soon, *inshallah.* Soon."

One rare and blessed day, when everybody was out of the house, Cindy and Mohammed found themselves alone. Nobody was listening, nobody was hovering on the other side of the wall, nobody was watching them going in and out of the bathroom. Soon afterward, Cindy knew she was pregnant.

They were planning to wait to have children, which had perplexed the family. It was a goal, as a nation, to build the population. How else could the country grow and become stronger? Nobody could understand why Cindy wasn't pregnant yet.

"What," Auntie Fatima said, "you don't want to have a baby now? You think you can just decide to have a baby, and you will have one?"

Mohammed had answered, "Isn't that what Allah said? Just ask, and Allah will give it to you!"

But Cindy and Mohammed were overjoyed knowing they would be blessed with their first child together. Then, the joy turned to fear. Cindy was bleeding. Mohammed took her to the hospital.

"Relax, Honey," he soothed. "It will be ok, *inshallah.*" But it wasn't ok. Suddenly, it felt like someone had punched Cindy in the stomach.

They called for the nurse, who came into the room and asked Cindy harshly, "What did you do?"

"They don't treat you with a very good bedside manner here, do they?" Cindy said to Mohammed. "Why would they say that to me?"

"They do that just to annoy me," he said. He was trying to keep Cindy calm, to keep her from feeling responsible for the miscarriage.

But it got worse. Mohammed had to leave. He was due back on base, the Army wouldn't allow him to take time off while tensions were high, and he had to go. The hospital required that he sign a paper – a blank paper. He and Cindy were both afraid. The hospital said they might have to do a D&C, but what else would they do to her? With a signed blank paper, they could do anything. But if Mohammed didn't sign? They would do nothing without the husband's signature.

They gave Cindy a pain medication, and as she fell asleep she heard her husband saying, "Take care of her! She is my life! I don't know what I would do without her!"

Later, when she awoke, the bleeding had stopped. There was no need for a D&C. She'd lost the baby. As she came to her senses, she could hear the hospital staff talking about Mohammed, mimicking his cries of, "She is my life!" Arab men do not openly dote on their wives; it is cause for ridicule and shaming.

When Cindy got home Zamzam was waiting. "Too much intimacy," she declared. "That is why you lose the baby."

Cindy would learn to live with the lack of privacy, with Zamzam's piercing eyes, tuned ears, and muttered comments which, even when she could not understand them, she knew were surely about her. Her mother-in-law's vigilance was accompanied by ceaseless, incomprehensible commentary. As time went on, and Cindy began to understand bits and pieces, it became obvious that Zamzam was a keen observer of everyone around her, always ready to compare, criticize, and point out injustices. This included the love lives of her sons, which she was not above commenting on.

One day she overheard Zamzam say, "Mohammed only has one wife. Other men, they have more wives, more intimacy. But Mohammed can only be with *her.*" She would never call Cindy by name. It was always just, *her.*

Oh, poor Mohammed! He deserved another wife! A local wife! Never mind that when Zamzam's own husband, Ali Mubarak, took a second wife it had upset Zamzam, enraged her. Her husband's second wife was a constant source of irritation, but when it came to Zamzam's son, he apparently deserved a second wife. Many men had an Emirati first wife, but also took foreign women as second, third, and sometimes fourth wives. Often, those women were from poor countries that had been ravaged by war, or their husbands were dead, and marriage to an Emirati was an escape from an impoverished life. Somehow Zamzam seemed to have ascribed this circumstance to Cindy. She saw Cindy, the foreign wife, as a refugee who was lucky that Mohammed had rescued her from misery.

Doesn't she realize what it means that I'm American? Cindy thought with outrage. *I come from an old, respectable Southern family. I am a southern belle! Not a refugee! I gave up a lot to come here!*

Mohammed's Auntie Fatima was conciliatory. "Never mind. Just spend all his money," she advised Cindy. "Don't let him get ahead. If he has extra money, then he can get another wife. If he is always poor, he cannot have more wives."

But Mohammed would never get another wife, she was sure of that. She knew him too well to worry about that. Besides, as far as Cindy was concerned, if Mohammed wanted another wife, well – then he wouldn't have her any more. She would be the only wife, or she would be gone.

Arab women were very matter-of-fact when joking about sex. Discussing it didn't embarrass them; the subject was no different than a discussion revolving around furniture, housemaids, or children. And whenever the ladies gathered, there was always a good joke to be made, often to Cindy's great embarrassment.

"Cindy, do you like *muz?*" one of the aunties would ask, picking up a banana. There were always bananas in the fruit basket, but when they said *"muz,"* it was with a lasciviousness that implied that they didn't mean the fruit. There was always laughter, and a lewd discussion of how big it was, how long, how thick.

God, Cindy thought, *all these old ladies do all day is sit around and talk about SEX!* It was embarrassing, to the point where Cindy couldn't bear to look at a banana. She couldn't utter the word for banana in Arabic. It caused her to blush crimson – it was also the word for penis. And to make things worse, there was a lady in the group who kept saying the word to Cindy, trying to get her to repeat it. Cindy didn't understand. Why would this lady make her say this?

"Why won't you say my name?" the lady finally asked. "Moza. What is the problem? You don't like my name?" She was just introducing herself, trying to be friendly. Cindy couldn't do it. She couldn't say that name. She didn't know that *muz* was simply "banana," and *Moza* was a girl's name, Arabic for "Grace." She couldn't say "banana" until long afterward, until she knew that there was an entirely different Arabic word for penis.

Mothers-in-law always loom large in the lives of new wives and Zamzam, despite her small stature, occupied a large space in Cindy's. How could she not? She was always nearby. But while Cindy was determined not to allow Zamzam's selfish bitterness and distrust to poison her marriage to Mohammed, she wondered what role Zamzam had played in the failure of Mohammed's first marriage, to Aisha.

Mohammed never wanted to discuss that marriage, and although she was curious, Cindy didn't push it. Why should she? They had so little time together anyway, she didn't want to spend it talking about his first wife. The one that had been such a shock to her. Truth be told, she was still working through her anger at not being told sooner. But the other truth was, she really liked Aisha. Aisha was always nice and friendly, and she bore no resentment toward Cindy. She didn't see her often but, as she got to know her, Cindy realized that Aisha had not been as good as Cindy at brushing off Zamzam's tirades. Tiny Zamzam had, indeed, been a weighty factor in the problems that lead to the end of that marriage.

Mohammed had once, Aisha confided to Cindy, struck her. *How can this be,* Cindy thought? This was not her gentle and caring Mohammed, the man she knew. Was it true? And if so, what could have provoked him to such an act? But Cindy now knew how manipulative Zamzam could be. And Mohammed was a young man of eighteen when he and Aisha had wed, not the mature twenty-six-year old Cindy had married. Aisha had been a child of fourteen. One of the few times that Mohammed did talk about Aisha, he revealed a clue.

"She said my mother is a thief," he said, and would say no more.

Cindy heard the story from Aisha a different way. "One day," Aisha told her, "My mother-in-law is behind me, in my house. She makes no noise, but suddenly she is there. I am startled! I think she is a thief!" And Cindy could picture it, even hear it.

Aisha: "What! You scare me! I think you are a thief!"

Zamzam: "Oh! She calls me a thief in my own son's house! Wait until Mohammed hears that his wife says this about me!"

Cindy could see how it could have happened. From Zamzam's point of view, it was Aisha who had caused problems for Zamzam. She had not been a good daughter-in-law, not considerate. She would not listen; she didn't do things for her. She quarreled. She had refused to live in the same house with her mother-in-law, which was a great insult and caused trouble in the marriage. A daughter-in-law should be there to help her husband's mother. Instead, stubborn Aisha had only made trouble, gossiping and complaining about Zamzam to others and to Mohammed.

Cindy didn't blame her one bit. Aisha wasn't really married to Mohammed, who was almost never around. She was married to Zamzam.

Aisha didn't hold a grudge against Cindy. She was probably grateful that Mohammed had met Cindy and decided initiate the divorce, because then Aisha could get out of the marriage. Divorce was much easier for the husband to initiate than the wife. To obtain a divorce against the husband's will, a wife had to go through a process in which she filed a petition for divorce, and then she could be granted the divorce if she provided a good reason, which might be that they hadn't had sex for three months, she could prove abuse, or the husband wasn't providing. The husband, on the other hand, needed only to repeat the words, "I divorce you, I divorce you, I divorce you." After a waiting period of three months, to ensure that the wife was not pregnant, he was free.

The divorce had cost Mohammed. When they married, Aisha had received a dowry, property and money, which she kept after the divorce. This explained why Mohammed didn't have any money, and why so many family members were living together under the same roof. Financially, he was starting over.

Zamzam wasn't upset about the divorce. She was always angry. Always looking to do battle. It was her personality. Unhappy. A victim of everyone, and everything. Zamzam's life consisted of an endless series of injustices. She would always play the part of the victim, claiming to be targeted by everyone else, who only wanted to make her life miserable.

And it wasn't only Cindy's problem. If a neighbor went somewhere, Zamzam expected to be invited to go. If they resisted, Zamzam could throw a tantrum and insist, getting into the car despite their protests. As time went on, they began to whisper to Cindy, as she sat beside the perpetually embattled Zamzam, *"How can you live with that woman?"* For Cindy, this question was the answer she'd been searching for. It wasn't her, or anything that she was doing, that was causing Zamzam to act as she did. It wasn't Cindy's problem at all. It was Zamzam's.

Cindy knew that she needed to keep the peace with her mother-in-law, however difficult, or even impossible, it might seem. She also knew that she must stay true to herself, and who she was. Try to become what Zamzam thought she should be? That was not possible; she already knew that no matter what she did, the woman would find something to criticize. Cindy could have been the Queen of England, and Zamzam would act the same. Zamzam was just a bitter, angry, and critical woman who created her own suffering. There would never be anything Cindy could do to change it. She could see, from the way others acted around Zamzam, and the things they said, that she was not the only one who suffered her criticism. She was not willing to lose herself. She could fit in, she could adapt. But she could not become a different person. She would not pretend to be someone she was not.

The best thing to do was to try to get along, and stay one step ahead of trouble. She would always call Mohammed and tell him what she was doing, so that he would never be caught off guard when Zamzam called to tattle on Cindy. She would help Zamzam out. She would treat her with respect. She would do things for her when needed, and even sometimes when she didn't ask for it. The rest didn't matter. She would never let Zamzam come between her and Mohammed. With that, Cindy let it go. Eventually they would move to Abu Dhabi. *Inshallah.*

From top: People remarked that Cindy looked like Princess Diana; dressed up as an Arab princess; in kohl eyeliner.

Chapter 8: Becoming Muslim

That first winter, the rainy season began in September and lasted until March. It rained, rained, and rained. Everybody said they'd never seen so much rain.

"You're lucky, Honey," Mohammed said. "We usually have some rain. This year, it rains cats and dogs!"

It rained for a couple of days, then it stopped. Then it rained some more. It was also surprisingly cold. She hadn't brought warm clothes, and the house had air conditioning, but no heat. She bought a sweater.

After the first rain cleansed the air, people put out bowls to gather the rainwater, which they used for drinking and ritual cleansing.

"It is Allah's water," Zamzam said. "Good water to wash for prayer." Cindy liked that. Pure and clean. Water from Heaven. Sometimes they did the same thing at home. She thought of the snow cream they made, growing up back in North Carolina. Mocksville was in the Piedmont just east of the Appalachians, about 800 feet above sea level. They usually had some snow in December, January, and February. When that happened, they would go out and get fresh snow, bring it into the house, put it with milk and sugar, and eat it like ice cream. You always knew not to do it from the first snow of the year, because that was cleaning the air out. Only the purest snow made good snow cream.

Sprigs of green began to pop out here and there, reminding her of North Carolina. The air smelled damp and fresh. It was a smell that comforted her, relieved the ache of homesickness. Year by year, it would rain less and less, but whenever it rained she would always breathe in and remember that smell, and how it made her feel. It would forever remind her of that soggy first year, and bring a pang of remembered homesickness.

The main roads were all flooded, unfit for driving. The side streets were soupy, unfit even for walking. She couldn't go out visiting without ruining her shoes. There was nothing to do but read. The problem was, Cindy couldn't find any books in English. They were unheard of in Khorfakkan; many of the older people couldn't read. They were illiterate. The books that were available in the shops were mostly religious, and they were all in Arabic.

Mohammed's brother Abdulrahman was the only person she knew who owned anything written in English. Abdul was smart. His job as a dispatcher for the local police required that he communicate with many people who spoke little or no Arabic, and he had picked up a working knowledge of several languages without formally studying them. Instead, he spoke with people and he read. He was fluent in Urdu, the language of Pakistan, and spoke very good English. In fact, his English was better than Mohammed's. He was a natural. Cindy had a lot of respect for Abdul. He had made her feel welcome. He had taken care of her that first day Mohammed was gone, sitting with her and the ladies, translating, then diagnosing her tears and curing them with sandwiches. Other than Mohammed and Auntie Fatima, Abdulrahman was her biggest supporter and she considered him a true friend. Whenever he was around, she talked with him as much as possible. And he loaned his books to her.

So, Cindy read. She read constantly, devouring everything Abdulrahman brought to her. Most of the books were religious – the Muslim religion says that everything that one does should praise Allah. If one reads, it should be the words of the Prophet or other words of religious instruction, the *hadiths*. Thus, out of necessity if not desire, Cindy's religious instruction began with an English translation of the Quran.

Far from home, family, and her own church, she read. Before long, she began noticing parallels between the Quran and her Bible. She knew the Bible well; she'd studied it every Wednesday evening for her entire life, right up until she married Mohammed. To her amazement, she found that the same stories were in the Quran. There they were, the Old Testament stories of Adam and Eve, Cain and Abel, Noah, Abraham, Lot, Joseph, Moses, Gideon, David and Goliath, Jonah and the whale. And there was the New Testament story of Jesus, Mary, and Joseph.

She began to compare the two books. When she came to a story in the Quran she read it, and then opened her own Bible to review the account of the same event. The similarities between the stories about Mary and the birth of baby Jesus were the most unexpected; she didn't know that Muslims believed in Jesus, but they did. There were only two things different. In the Quran, there was no Joseph to step in as Mary's husband and surrogate father to Jesus and, more importantly, it was clearly stated that Jesus was not the son of God. Cindy realized that the many Arab women she'd met who were named Maryam were named after Mary of the Bible, the mother of Jesus. The Quran said that Jesus was sent by God to be a great prophet, that he was given the Gospel from God, and that someday he would arise, alive. But it was not suitable, not possible, that God should father a son.

Muslims believed many of the same things that she, as a Christian, did – except, and this was a big exception – they did not believe that Jesus was the son of God. They believed that there was only one God and that God was one being, not three, as in the Holy Trinity.

It was mid-December. They had just celebrated the UAE's 11th National Day with a parade and fireworks display. The town was decorated everywhere with the red, green, white, and black colors of the national flag. Seeing the red and green made Cindy feel little less homesick. She wouldn't be celebrating Christmas this year because her new Muslim family celebrate the birth of Jesus. There were some Christians living in Khorfakkan, and they could worship and celebrate Christmas. She saw the familiar decorations here and there, but not many.

It doesn't matter, she told herself. *You can't feel sorry for yourself. You made your decision, and you live with it.* She would appreciate all that she had, and not mourn what she had given up. She was meant to be here. It was God's plan.

Cindy soon found out that God indeed had other plans than for her to worry about missing Christmas. Instead of celebrating a birth, Cindy would learn about mourning the dead. In two short weeks, Cindy would learn everything about Muslim funerals. On December 12th, Moza, the lady whose banana-like name she would not say for the first few months, suddenly died.

Moza was be buried according to Islamic *sharia* law. Her *Janaza,* or funeral, commenced immediately with the washing of her body by the female members of her immediate family. The body was then wrapped in a white shroud.

Cindy went with the women of Mohammed's family to Moza's house. Mohammed was on base and couldn't get away. She listened while they read the *Salat al Janaza,* the funeral prayer for forgiveness of the dead. Moza would be buried later that day, and for the next few days, friends and relatives would come to visit and offer their condolences to her husband and family.

Cindy was sad. She liked funny Moza the banana lady, and she grieved her loss. She wondered if Moza had an undiagnosed illness – high blood pressure, perhaps, or a heart condition. People didn't go to the doctor for regular checkups; they only went if they felt ill. When something happened, they asked God's forgiveness and blessing, and they praised Him, saying *"Allahu akbar."* God is greatest. Everything that happened in life, even death, was God's will. Praise God.

Automobile accidents were common, often deadly. One of the first things that Cindy had noticed when she moved to the UAE was the crazy driving. There was no other way to describe it. Most of the drivers were men, and everyone seemed to be in a hurry to get where they were going. Maybe they wished to be the fastest car on the road. The first automobiles had appeared only a couple of decades earlier, and back then there were few roads. So, they drove cross country at the highest speed possible, following the camel tracks, careening over the endlessly drifting sands. This habit was passed on to the next generation, to young men who were driving faster, more powerful cars on paved highways. It was not unusual for Cindy to be driving along and see a car speeding up in her rear-view mirror, lights flashing, almost running her off the road as it swerved around to pass before she even knew what had happened. The ones who didn't pass honked and tailgated until she pulled aside. And nobody wore seat belts.

One rainy afternoon, just a week after Moza's funeral, Abdulrahman's houseboy came running over. "Accident! Abdulrahman killed!" Despite the rain, Cindy immediately set off for Auntie Fatima's house. She didn't want to believe it. A car pulled up, and the driver offered her a ride. He clearly knew who she was and where she was going, and without hesitation, Cindy got into the car.

"Who brought you here?" one of Mohammed's cousins asked when she arrived.

"Someone stopped and asked me if I wanted a ride. I don't know who it was. He asked me if this was where I was headed and when I said yes, he said to get in."

"How could you ride with someone you do not know?" the cousin cried. Under no circumstances should a lady accept a ride from a strange man. It was a scandal.

Cindy brushed it off. "I was in a hurry to get here!" She didn't know him, but he obviously knew who she was. What difference did it make in an emergency like this?

"Did you call Mohammed?" Cindy asked someone.

"We have been trying. He is not there. They say he is already coming to Khorfakkan."

"Does he know what's happened?"

"No."

Mohammed had left the base early because a group of his friends who were at the language school in Charlotte, guys that Cindy had met when she and Mohammed were dating, were coming over to welcome Cindy to the UAE. Just as he pulled up in front of the house, the ambulance arrived. Mohammed ran toward it, screaming, "What happened? Who is it?" It devastated Cindy to see Mohammed so anguished.

Ordinarily it would have been Mohammed's duty, but because of the violence of the accident, Abdulrahman's body was washed and shrouded at the morgue instead of by the men in his family. People came to pray over it. There were four *Salut al Janaza,* prayers said in the presence of the shrouded body, as required. Then, that same day, the body was taken in procession to be buried in a cemetery. The grave was dug perpendicular to Mecca, and Abdulrahman's body was laid on its right side so that he would be facing in the direction of prayer. The grave was marked with a simple stone, turned to stand on end, but no more than twelve inches high. They received visitors for three days. They grieved. But they did so with quiet dignity. It was not acceptable to weep and sob loudly.

To say that Cindy would miss Abdulrahman would not begin to describe her grief. She was grateful that she didn't have to face Christmas. She was too shattered. When Shaukat and the other Pakistanis had moved out, Abdulrahman went to visit them and he had written a letter to Cindy from Pakistan, in English. It had touched her heart then, and she had saved the letter, kept it in a safe place. Now, she got it out and read it. This treasured memento of Abdulrahman meant even more than it had.

With Abdulrahman gone, Cindy inherited the book collection he left behind. She read. Her interest in Islam increased. She began to think about converting. The three main religions, she reasoned, Judaism, Christianity, and Islam, all came from the same place. So of course, there would be similarities. The people were the same, and the stories were the same. It was just how people had interpreted them that had changed.

Through her reading of the Quran and Abdul's religious books, and her observations of the Muslim community surrounding her and how the people conducted themselves, Cindy felt increasingly drawn to the religion. She realized that their faith was everything to them; they didn't make a move in life without thinking that God was watching them. To tell a lie was a sin against God, and not to be taken lightly. These people, she thought, are honest, good, nice people. The Quran laid everything out about how to live a good and holy life. Their daily expressions of greeting, gratitude, hope, and satisfaction reflected the very same sentiments about God that she'd heard growing up in the Baptist church.

But for Muslims, there was no preacher in the pulpit. There was no judge but God. As a Muslim, she could live her life in a way that made her, and her alone, responsible for her relationship with God and, in the end, it was up to God to judge her, and no one else. There were no preachers to confess to when she'd sinned, and to decide how and when she should be punished. No preachers to condemn her, to tell her to repent, to say she must be saved from damnation by proclaiming here on

Earth that she was a sinner. It was up to God to judge her, up to God to condemn her, or forgive her.

Cindy tentatively began to read the *hadiths*, the prayers and interpretations of the words of the Prophet, in Abdul's books. The *hadiths* were reports written after the Prophet's time, and they described and interpreted the words in the Quran. They were written by religious scholars, all men. There were instructions on every aspect of life, including when and how to pray, what to eat and drink (never eat pork, never drink alcohol) and that women must be modestly dressed when in the company of someone other than their husband, brother, or father. The Quran instructed women to cover, and the *hadith* described how it should be done. They should cover their heads including all their hair, which was a symbol of sensuality and beauty, their arms, and their legs including the ankle. Everything but her face and her hands.

Cindy had already begun wear the Arab *hijab,* covering her hair as a sign of unity with her husband and respect for his religious customs. She liked the idea that Mohammed, and only Mohammed, would see her hair uncovered. It also made her feel that she fit in more with the locals. Her white skin set her apart; everyone knew who she was – Mohammed's American wife, the local celebrity – even though she didn't know them. But with her head covered, she felt more anonymous, and she was treated a bit more like one of them. She also found an added benefit – it protected her fine, soft hair from the harsh and drying elements. She ordered tailored dresses with long skirts and sleeves that covered her legs and arms. This protected her skin, as well, from the searing sun and wind-driven sand. Soon, she discovered the usefulness of the *abaya,* the black cloak that women wore over their clothes when they went out. It was the cloak that Zamzam had worn when they first met. Cindy could throw on jeans and a t-shirt and if she needed to go out, just cover up with an *abaya.* She could even go out in her pajamas if she had to. And she never had to worry about how her hair looked.

Thinking about the words of the Quran objectively, Cindy knew that they could be interpreted in other, less restrictive, less conservative ways. It was possible to argue that women were not instructed to cover their heads. Interpreted literally, the words in the Quran did not carry that meaning at all. But the tradition of covering had evolved, and at least in the UAE, it was still flexible. Women covered, but to different degrees.

The most modest women covered not just their hair, but their hands and their faces as well, with black gloves and *niqabs,* veils with eye slits, or sheet veils that they simply threw over their heads to cover their entire faces while still being able to see through, however dimly. Cindy liked to think that those women were covering completely out of religiosity, because they wanted to be as close to God as possible. But she knew that wasn't always the case. There were women whose husbands insisted they cover. It was a form of control.

Five times a day Cindy heard the *adhan,* the Islamic call to prayer, echo from mosque to mosque. It was always at a slightly different time, adjusted each day according to the changing position of the sun in the sky. The *muezzin*'s melodious voice would chant the phrases: "*Allahu Akbar, God is Greatest ... I bear witness that there is no deity except God ... Mohammed is the messenger of God ... Come to prayer ... Come to success ... God is Greatest ... There is no deity except God ...*" The simple prayer, said five times a day, was preceded by a ritual cleansing which must be performed to go before Allah. Men stopped what they were doing and gathered together in mosques, which were scattered throughout the cities, towns, and villages so that one was never more than a few minutes' walk away. Most women prayed at home.

Cindy began to pray on her own, secretly. In addition to the words, there were prescribed movements – standing, bending down, and kneeling, head touching the ground. She learned to use the Arabic words for 'God bless you' *(Baraka Allahu fika),* 'God knows what's best' *(Allahu A'lam),* 'Trust in God' *(Tawakkalna ala Allah),* 'God forgive me' *(Astaghfiru lillah),* and 'Thank you God' *(Ashokrulillah)* in daily conversation.

One weekend, Cindy confided her thoughts to Mohammed. "I want to convert. I want to become a Muslim."

"No, no," Mohammed said. "It is too soon. Don't rush into this. You have been here less than one year. It is too soon." How could she be sure that this was right for her? Many men who married foreign women pressured them to convert. If the wife didn't want to convert, it created trouble in the marriage. Women who married Arab men and converted to Islam for the wrong reasons always regretted it, feeling trapped and confused. This was happening to Colleen, Cindy's British friend who had married Ahmed. Mohammed knew that, if Cindy converted, there was no changing her mind, no denouncing the faith. Once a Muslim, always a Muslim.

"But you haven't pressured me about this," Cindy pointed out. "It's something that I've decided to do. I came to this decision on my own. Nobody pressured me. Not, you, not Abdulrahman, not anybody."

"I know," Mohammed said. "I told Abdulrahman not to push it with you. You are as stubborn as a bull, and if he pushes you, it will backfire. You will want to do the opposite. So, I tell him to lay off."

Cindy smiled sadly, thinking of Abdulrahman. He had answered her questions, he had told her what a great religion he thought it was, the best. He loved his religion, but he respected her Christianity and had never made her feel pressure to convert.

"This is a big decision," Mohammed said. "Take your time. Keep reading."

If she converted, Cindy would do it right. She was a good Christian. If she converted she would be a good Muslim. That meant wearing the *abaya* and *shayla* in public, praying five times each day, and observing all Muslim holy days and customs. If she converted, it would be for the right reasons. Mohammed hadn't pressured her; he would never force or coerce her into anything. She was following her own heart, the same heart that had led her to marry Mohammed. Now, she prayed to God once again. He had shown her that Mohammed was right for her by strengthening her love during the months of Mohammed's absence and silence. It was this same God that she would always pray to, whether she converted or not.

Weeks went by, and Cindy pondered her decision. She thought about Mohammed's family. They had accepted her without any pressure to convert. Some people still talked, said things, criticized. But that was true anywhere. She knew she was an outsider, an American, and converting would never change that. If she converted, would it change anything with Zamzam? With people who didn't like her, or didn't like the way she did things? Probably not, and she didn't care. She was who she was, Cindy Lou Davis, and she wasn't changing. If people liked her, fine. If not, that was their choice.

Mohammed was the only one who mattered, and he loved and accepted her just as she was. He'd already proven that he was there to support and protect her every step of the way. This was her decision, one that nobody would talk her into, or out of. This was between her and God. Their children, when they had them, would be Muslim. Their father's religion. So, there it was. God was telling her to go ahead. She was ready.

A few weeks later, they went to the court, where Cindy made her *shahaadah,* the formal declaration of faith, which was registered with the government. "Now you must abide by the Islamic law that you have chosen," the official said. And so, without ceremony, without celebration, without congregation, without consecration, it was done. Cindy Lou Davis became a Muslim.

Khorfakkan beach, 1984

El Paso, 1985

Denver, December 1986. Aminah was born one month later.

Cindy and Mohammed at the Dead Sea in Jordan with Aisha and Aminah, 1990

Dressed as Bedouins at Kan Zaman village, Jordan

Chapter 9: Building a Family

1985

"Honey, I have some news," Mohammed said one day when he telephoned from the base. "They are sending us to Texas for military training."

"Texas! Where?"

"Fort Bliss."

"That's in El Paso!" Cindy could hardly believe it. The only place outside North Carolina where she'd ever dreamed of living. They were going to be stationed there. Once again, when something was meant to be, it would be. After living in the UAE for three years, Cindy would see her family again. They would be out of the crowded house, she would no longer be under Zamzam's watchful eye, and she and Mohammed would have their own place.

When Cindy left home and family in 1982, she was an inexperienced young bride, just twenty years old. Three years later, she emerged from the plane as a happily married and confident young Muslim American woman, wearing jeans and a *hijab*.

In the housing on the base, she found herself in a community of other young women with whom she had much in common. Some of the men, like Mohammed, had brought wives along, and most of them spoke Arabic and some English. They, like Cindy, were eager to improve their skills. Their almost daily get-togethers became informal language lessons. In El Paso, and later when they were transferred to Denver, Cindy had the opportunity to learn to speak Arabic without embarrassment, with the encouragement of women who were just like her.

In Khorfakkan, immersed in a new language and culture without anyone to translate, Cindy had begun to understand and speak Arabic but had to guess the meaning. Sometimes she thought she knew a word or phrase only to be embarrassed to find that she had confused two similar words. When she got a new car, a cousin congratulated her with *"Mabrouk!"* When Cindy responded, *"Mubarak al aik,"* thinking she was saying something like, "God willed this blessing upon me," the cousin burst out laughing. Cindy later found out, to her embarrassment, that she had said, "May Mubarak be upon you." Mubarak was a man's name. She had called for a man to be on top her cousin!

In the United States, away from the custom of separating men and women, the young couples hung out together, watching movies or just sitting and talking. Cindy, as the American *hijabi* wife, had celebrity status. Everyone wanted to have the closest ties to Cindy. "We are from the same place, so we have the closest ties to Cindy ..." "No, no. Her husband is related to my husband, so I am closer ..." Cindy and Mohammed laughed about it. If you were related to the American, no matter how distant the connection, the higher your status.

When Mohammed had leave, he went back to the UAE to visit his family while Cindy went to North Carolina to spend time with hers. They saw that she was happy, and they could clearly see her deep love for Mohammed. Gladys and R.G.'s comfort with the marriage and with Mohammed grew. But in town, outside of her family home, people who didn't know Cindy stared at her *hijab*. She was the local girl who had betrayed her upbringing, committed a terrible sin. After a couple of days, unwilling to endure stares and looks of contempt, she quit wearing the *hijab* around Mocksville. The tiny, insular little town wasn't used to foreigners.

Living in the bigger, more multicultural cities, El Paso and later Denver, her *hijab* was sometimes the subject of a curious question – "Why do you wear that?" – but not outright disapproval. But in El Paso and Denver, people still sometimes assumed that Cindy, wearing her *hijab* and walking beside Mohammed, was a foreigner.

"You speak very good English," someone might say.

"She should," Mohammed would speak up. "She's American!" It was always good for a laugh.

The second year, in Denver, Cindy became pregnant and gave birth to a baby girl. Cindy's sister Linda was there for the birth, and her mother arrived the next day. "Oh," Gladys said when she saw the baby. "she has dark skin!" The worry that Gladys had felt when Cindy and Mohammed married had given way to a growing love and respect for Mohammed. She, and all the rest of Cindy's family, were thrilled with the new baby, and they loved her beautiful skin – but none more than Cindy herself.

"She's exactly what I was wishing for," she told her mother. "Remember those kids I used to babysit? The ones whose father was part Cherokee? They had this beautiful dark skin and I always said, when I had kids, I wanted them to have skin like that." Cindy and Mohammed named her Aminah, after Mohammed's most elderly auntie.

After three years in the United States, Mohammed's training was finished. It was time to move back to Khorfakkan with their six-month-old baby girl. They packed up their belongings and piled everything into a trailer. R.G. flew out to Denver, and he and Mohammed drove to North Carolina while Cindy and the baby flew. For the whole trip, Mohammed entertained R.G. with his sense of humor and funny use of American slang. Just as Cindy had hoped when they got married, that road trip created a lasting bond between Mohammed and his father-in-law.

In El Paso and in Denver, Mohammed called Cindy by her pet name so often that sometimes people thought "Honey" was her real name. Arab people who knew Cindy well called her "Sindiya." Now Cindy had a new Arab name – "Umm Aminah" – Aminah's mother.

Exiting the plane into the enormous, shiny new terminal in Dubai, it seemed that everything had changed. The UAE was nearing the end of the first stage growth and modernization. When oil was discovered in the Persian Gulf in the early 20th century, it had brought wealth to Iraq, Kuwait, and Saudi Arabia, and to the oil companies in control, but did nothing to change the squalid conditions for the struggling tribes living in poverty in the nearby Trucial States. For years, the Trucial States – the future UAE – had languished as neighboring oil-rich countries built cities with modern shipping facilities and airports. Without the resources that oil money brought, the ruling sheikhs clashed over land and sovereignty, and their people lived as they had for hundreds of years.

Eventually, a group of sheikhs formed an alliance that brought stability to the region, and transportation improved with better roads, the availability of vehicles, and the advent of air travel. The rulers of Abu Dhabi and Dubai began to visit other Persian Gulf countries and were amazed at what they saw. Why didn't they have these modern amenities? Why were their people living without electricity, without fresh water, in homes without solid walls? In the 1950's, when Mohammed was born in the cave in Khorfakkan, Abu Dhabi was no more than a collection of *barasti* huts in the sand. There was no school, no hospital. There were no toilets – that business was done on the beach. Dubai, older and more developed, was a center of trade thanks to its natural harbor but the oil fields in the Persian Gulf owned by neighboring countries had done little to grow that economy.

The discovery of oil off the coast of Abu Dhabi in 1960 brought the unimaginable wealth that changed everything. After centuries barely surviving on pearling, fishing, trading, growing dates and raising camels, the Trucial States were united as a new country under Sheikh Zayed in 1971. The leader had proclaimed that in ten years there would be hospitals and schools in every Emirate. There would be great, green cities. Abu Dhabi would be the seat of government and Dubai would be the financial center. They would become world-class capitals, and in time the smaller cities and towns would be developed and modernized. All Emirati people, even those in the desert and remote villages, would live in houses on land provided by the government. Now, it was all happening. Even when oil prices fell, as they had in the 1980's, and would again in the future, growth and progress would continue in the UAE for decades.

At the Port of Fujairah, the original plan for construction which began in 1978 and completed in 1983 had been enlarged to include expanded facilities for oil and fuel shipping. Paved roads and traffic circles, complete with fountains and flowery landscaping, were replacing dirt roads and chaos. Main roads were lit at night. Products from Great Britain, France, and the United States now sat on shelves alongside foods and sundries from Oman, Saudi Arabia, Iran, Lebanon, and India. Shopping centers with designated parking spaces were under construction as were buildings several stories high, including a large, modern hospital in Fujairah. There were not one, but three television stations from Dubai. Most of the local Emirati people had moved into cinderblock houses with modern conveniences, leaving their old historic villages to deteriorate. Cindy had been the second woman in Khorfakkan to drive, but now women drivers were a common sight.

Cindy wanted to get back in touch with her English friend Colleen, who had moved to Abu Dhabi with Ahmed while Cindy and Mohammed were in the United States. She considered driving to Abu Dhabi to visit, but hesitated when Mohammed told her that he'd heard they were having marital problems.

"I don't want you to get involved in it, Honey," Mohammed said. "I think you should not go."

Cindy didn't know what the trouble was; she could only imagine. Colleen was idealistic. She had met Ahmed and fallen in love with the idea of an exotic, oil-rich Arabia, a combination of old-world romance and 20th-century luxury. She'd imagined living in a modern-day palace, lounging in the Arabian sun. But the reality was far different. Khorfakkan had been rainy, cold, rocky, muddy. Familiar and comforting items, like British biscuits and tea, were impossible to get. Their house was cold and damp. There was little privacy from the family.

This happened often. Western women would arrive, only to find that the reality didn't match the Arab life in their dreams. The husband who had been loving and devoted before marriage would reveal his conservative side upon arrival in the Middle East, pressuring his wife to convert to Islam, and putting restrictions on her wardrobe and activities. Meanwhile the wife, who had expected to further liberalize her new husband, found him to be more religious than she had realized, more demanding, his views more intractable.

Families could be critical and unaccepting, and sometimes young foreign wives abandoned their very identities to try to please them and fit in. They converted to Islam for the wrong reasons, and then struggled to pray, struggled to believe. They questioned everything about themselves, their faith, their relationships, their lives. They tried to pray more, to pray harder, more fervently, more often. It didn't work, because they weren't doing it for the right reasons. They were trying to please a husband and his family. They were trying to be something that they were not.

Colleen and Abdul were living in Abu Dhabi, where there was a growing expat community. Colleen would be making friends with whom she had much more in common than with her husband – people from the U.K. who socialized as couples, who threw posh dinners, who drank champagne at Friday brunch, who celebrated Christmas. It was easy to imagine them growing apart.

Cindy didn't go to Abu Dhabi to visit Colleen, and they lost touch. Eventually she heard from Mohammed that Colleen and Ahmed had divorced, Colleen had moved back to England, and that she had been diagnosed with cancer. Cindy wondered about their son. He'd been born in England, before they were married. Had Ahmed allowed her to take the boy with her to England? Or had he insisted that the boy stay in the UAE, and be raised as a Muslim? Had Colleen been forced to flee to keep her son? Cindy could imagine the legal struggle they might be in, with Colleen revealing the forged marriage license. Or maybe she had just let him go. Maybe they had worked something out, but Cindy never knew what happened – if Colleen had survived her cancer, and what became of Ahmed and their son. It all just seemed to blow away, into the desert.

In the three years since they left, so many things had changed but in one way, nothing had changed. Cindy found herself living in the same house, Mohammed's house, sharing it with his family. Again. There was tiny Zamzam, with the bigger-than-life temper. There was Mohammed's father, Ali Mubarak, divorced from the second wife. It hadn't worked out; perhaps Zamzam had something to do with that? There was Mohammed's daughter Maryam, and his youngest son Ahmed. Mohammed's younger brother Hassan Ali and his wife, Aisha, were living in Mohammed's other house, the one he had bought for his mother, with Mohammed's two older sons. Hassan was still a child, always depending on others to tell him how to do things.

"Sindiya," he would call to say, "Come change the light bulb. I do not know how."

Emirati people didn't know how to do anything around the house. They had lived so simply for so long that they knew nothing about construction, electricity, or plumbing. Whenever anything broke or needed replacing, they called someone. They had the money to pay for it, and there were plenty of men coming from Pakistan, India, wherever, ready to claim that they knew what to do – whether they did or not – and take the money. There was really no such thing as a professional tradesman. They claimed a profession when they filled out the paperwork for a visa. Nobody checked. Nobody knew the difference.

But Cindy knew better. She was raised in a do-it-yourself American family alongside four brothers, who she made sure she kept up with. She knew how to do things around the house. Even if she didn't have the skills or the tools to do something, she knew when it was done right. Or wrong. Now she wanted her own house, where her children could have their own rooms, she could fix things up the way she wanted, and she and Mohammed would have privacy on weekends. Their plan was still to move to Abu Dhabi, but circumstances kept getting in the way. It was always a money problem. At first, he was paying debts from his divorce, and then Hassan had gotten married, and Mohammed had to help him pay the dowry. Now Hassan was divorcing his first wife Aisha, and marrying again. His new wife was Fatima. Mohammed was helping with the expenses.

Of course, Zamzam had opinions Hassan's wives. Neither of them every did anything for Zamzam. Nobody did. Although Cindy now had two Arab names, Zamzam still refused to say either of them. It was always "she," "her," or "your wife" never "Sindiya" or "Umm Aminah." It wasn't that she blamed Cindy for Mohammed's divorce from Aisha. No, Zamzam herself had done everything she could to break that marriage up. Zamzam had arranged the marriage, but by the end of the first year, Aisha could do nothing right. It didn't matter who was with her sons, she wasn't going to be happy. She would always try to break up the marriage so that they could get a better wife. She did it to Cindy, she had done it to Abdulrahman's wife, Maryam, she had done it with Hassan's first wife, and soon she would be doing it to Fatima.

Abdulrahman's widow Maryam had taken the opportunity, after his death, to distance herself from the family and escape from Zamzam. Aisha, Mohammed's first wife, was still young enough to get married again. She and her second husband, another Mohammed Ali, would eventually have eight children.

A year after returning from Denver, Cindy and Mohammed were expecting a second child. When they had come home with Aminah, Mohammed's family had commented on Aminah's dark skin. "Oh," they had said to Cindy, "she would be prettier if she looked like you." Cindy had one girl who looked like Mohammed. Now she found herself hoping for another girl – one who looked like her.

The house was already crowded. The government was providing more land and financing, and Mohammed had an opportunity to buy another house, where they would have room for their growing family. The new house was on the other side of Khorfakkan, in the new section near Auntie Fatima's house. Cindy liked the idea of moving closer to Fatima. Whereas Zamzam still complained about Cindy, and told people things that weren't true, Fatima said only nice things about Cindy. When Fatima talked about "Umm Aminah," it made people want to meet her. Auntie Fatima treated Cindy like a daughter – the same as her own daughters, Fatima, Maryam, and Aisha. *Oh,* Cindy often thought, *how I wish Fatima were my mother-in-law instead of Zamzam! They're so different. How can they be sisters?*

Cindy was looking forward to finally having her own house. There would be more space, and the best part would be escaping from Zamzam's constant presence. But her enthusiasm was quashed when she discovered that not only were she and Mohammed moving to the new house, but the rest of the family was moving with them. Hassan and his wife were getting their own house, but Zamzam, Ali, and the stepchildren were all moving into the new house with Cindy and Mohammed.

Cindy confronted Mohammed. "Why is everybody coming with us?" she fumed. "Let them have the new house, then. I'm tired of living with a houseful of people!" She would have been perfectly happy staying in the smaller house in the old area, if the others were gone.

"No, no!" Mohammed protested. "Honey, I am buying the new house for you!" He couldn't let her stay in the old house. People were leaving the old neighborhood, which was becoming run down, turning into a second-rate neighborhood for foreign workers – laborers and tradesmen from India and Pakistan. She couldn't stay there, but neither could his parents. He couldn't reject his family by refusing to bring them into the new neighborhood.

There was no way out of it; nothing to do but accept it. At least things were a little better for Cindy in the new house. She had a big bedroom, with her own refrigerator and television. Best of all, she had her own bathroom. No more sharing the bathroom with the whole family. She realized that Mohammed was doing the best he could. He was taking care of her, but he was also responsible for the well-being of the others. He would always cooperate with them, he would always strive to do right by them, to do what they wanted. He didn't make waves. He didn't rock the boat. And neither would she. After all, when things settled down and there was enough money, they would move to Abu Dhabi, *inshallah*. That was still the deal.

The new baby was another girl – and again, Cindy got what she wanted. This baby had the Davis fair skin. But when naming time came, there was a dilemma. Cindy had sworn that she would never name a daughter Aisha. Mohammed's first wife was Aisha. Cindy and Aisha liked each other, but why give your daughter the same name as your husband's ex-wife? And then there was the story of Aisha, who was widely said to be the favorite of the Prophet's many wives after the death of his beloved first wife, and was reported to be central to the irresolvable conflicts that had developed between the Sunni and the Shia Muslims. When yet another of Mohammed's cousins had died in a car crash – they were all too frequent – his young son asked where his father was. Hassan's first wife Aisha had told the boy, "Your father is in hell." Cindy was horrified. *How can she say such a thing?* And she swore again, *I will never have an Aisha!*

No, she didn't want an Aisha; they were nothing but trouble. But without thinking it through, they had named Aminah after one of Mohammed's two most elderly aunties. The only way to balance the honor was to name the second daughter after the other one – Auntie Aisha.

And so, Cindy had an Aisha.

Chapter 10: Desert Storm

1990

It was summer, and they were in Jordan for military training. It was a chance for Cindy to get out of Khorfakkan for a while, for her and Mohammed to spend time with their babies together as a family. One weekend, they took a trip down to the Dead Sea. Because Jordan was a country of Christian, Jewish and Muslim religions, Cindy did not wear the *abaya,* choosing instead to wear her favorite dress, beautiful bright green with embroidery from top to bottom, with a *hijab* to cover her head. It was her favorite dress.

On the way, they took in the views of the Holy Land and the valley of the River Jordan from Mount Nebo. They stopped in the town of Madaba to see the famous Byzantine mosaic map of Palestine and the Nile delta. Arriving at the Dead Sea lookout, it was crowded with tourists. Cindy found a bench and sat holding Aisha, who was being fussy. A woman who looked Asian sat down beside them. Speaking very carefully, she said to Cindy in perfect English, "Your-dress-is-ve-ry-beau-ti-ful."

She thinks I'm Arab! Cindy smiled. She was tempted to play with the woman's head. *Should I blow her mind and come back in English with a Southern accent?* People never realized that she was American, because she didn't dress in Western clothing. It would be so much fun to see the woman's surprise. But she didn't want to embarrass the poor lady. Keeping her secret to herself, she simply said, "Thank you."

During the day, Mohammed's training was at the base, but he came back to the hotel in Amman each night. Cindy spent her mornings taking the babies for walks in the city, before the sun became insufferably hot. For the rest of the day, she watched television and read any English language newspapers she could get her hands on, always thirsty for the latest news, more information. The Iran-Iraq war was finally ending, but now tensions were mounting over the price of oil, and

Iraq had pointed the finger at Kuwait and the UAE, who were producing more than their quotas. The falling prices were cutting into Iraqi oil profits and Iraq's president Saddam Hussein was complaining. Cindy wondered where it would lead.

In mid-July, when the military training ended, they went back to Khorfakkan and Cindy prepared to fly home to North Carolina with the babies. Mohammed called to tell her that Saddam Hussein had made several statements threatening Kuwait and the UAE, and had named the United States as well.

"He says the policies of some Arab rulers are American," Mohammed reported, "and that America wants to undermine Arab interest and security. He says, 'Cutting necks is better than cutting means of living.' And he warns that if his words fail to protect Iraqis, something will be done."

"What do you think is going to happen?"

"Our leaders say Saddam will probably not attack any time soon," Mohammed said. "It is okay for you to go home, *inshallah.*" The plan was to stay for about a month.

Cindy arrived home on the evening of August second and, after putting the babies to bed, she turned on the television, a treat she'd been looking forward to ever since she and Mohammed had returned to the UAE from Denver. If there was one thing she missed the most, other than family, it was American television. Morning shows, soap operas, game shows, the news – she loved it all, but she especially missed getting the news. Every time something happened, she always found out about it after the fact, which drove her crazy.

"To all intents and purposes, Kuwait has ceased to exist as an independent sovereign nation," anchor Ted Koppel announced at the beginning the ABC Nightline News, "and with one stroke, Saddam Hussein and Iraq have eliminated billions of dollars' worth of debts, acquired enormous amounts of oil resources on top of those already controlled, gained access to an important Persian Gulf port, and intimidated every other country in the region …"

Cindy sat dazed, taking it in. Unbelievable. Saddam Hussein had attacked Kuwait!

"… it is difficult to find anyone putting forth realistic counter measures that could force Iraqi troops out of Kuwait before they are good and ready to leave … Hussein appears to have gambled, and won."

Iraq and Kuwait had been in dispute over oil reserves and drilling near their shared border, and Iraq had demanded $10 billion from Kuwait to cover lost revenue from an oil field that it claimed Kuwait had drilled into. When Kuwait countered with an offer of $9 billion, Saddam Hussein had launched a full-scale attack. Within twelve hours, the Kuwaiti royal family had fled. It had all happened while she was in the air.

That night Cindy could hardly sleep, thinking. What would happen? In the morning, she could hardly wait to turn on the television. Stunned leaders from all over the region were meeting. The Arab League of Nations called an emergency meeting. The collective shock was apparent, but they stopped short of condemning the attack, instead adopting a "wait and see" attitude. Their decision was, for the time being, to do nothing. To wait and see. Were they afraid of Saddam Hussein? Meanwhile, the United Nations Security Council met, and voted to condemn the invasion. President George H.W. Bush issued an executive order freezing Iraqi and Kuwaiti assets in the U.S. and banning the import of oil from Iraq. Kuwait asked for military action.

"We would like to have military assistance in order to survive," the Kuwaiti representative said. "The U.S. intervention at this stage is of paramount importance."

If Iraq persisted, and this escalated, the UAE and the United States would surely become involved. Mohammed was in the Army. Cindy called him at the base, and they talked hurriedly, not wanting to waste a second of the precious, expensive long-distance telephone call.

"What do you think is going to happen?"

"God only knows," Mohammed said. "We have to wait and see. I can only tell you, Honey, travel is very dangerous right now. I don't know when it will be safe for you to come back."

In the coming days, when she wasn't busy with the babies or doing something with family, Cindy followed the news. There was a new 24-hour television news station, Cable News Network. If she woke up in the middle of the night, which she often did because of jet lag and the eight-hour time difference between Khorfakkan and home, she tuned in to CNN to find out if anything had happened. She was as close to obsessed as any young mother with two babies in diapers could be. CNN was using new satellite technology to report on the conflict, and people all over the world, including Cindy, could see live pictures as CNN reporters stood with the damage in Kuwait City as a backdrop. Meetings were being held around the world as leaders tried to figure out how to deal with the crisis.

Throughout August, Cindy remained in North Carolina, going to church and enjoying the family dinners. Gladys was ecstatic to have the two little girls to fuss over – Aminah, who looked like Mohammed, and Aisha, who was turning out to be the spitting image not of Cindy, but of Uncle Randy. What a relief it was, Cindy thought, to be out of the searing heat of summer in the Middle East. Everything was green, the flowers and shrubs were refreshed regularly by thunderstorms and showers, and she had the comfort of being surrounded by everything American, everything she had been craving.

If only the situation in the Middle East would improve. But it didn't. The economic sanctions placed on Iraq had little effect, and Saddam Hussein was proposing solutions that involved not only Kuwait but also Israel and the Palestinian Territory, trying to broaden his influence. In late August, Saddam appeared on television with a little boy from the U.K. who was a passenger on a British Airways flight that had landed in Kuwait earlier that month. All the passengers on the plane were removed and had been "guests" of the Iraqi government ever since. Cindy realized, with a shock, that it was the same flight she'd been on a week earlier, when they had landed in Kuwait on their way to North Carolina. It was terrifying to think what a close call it had been. She and her daughters could have been among those hostages.

Meanwhile, the local newspaper, the Davie County Enterprise Record, called and asked for an interview. Cindy was the local celebrity who had married an Arab and moved to the Middle East. The paper wanted to know what she thought was going to happen.

"We just have to wait and see," she said. "Saddam Hussein can't be allowed to gain control over everything, all the oil. He must be stopped, somehow. I hope they can convince him to pull his troops out of Kuwait. I hope there won't be a war, with the United States getting involved. But I don't know."

It was three months before Mohammed decided that it was safe for Cindy and the babies to fly home. Although there had been much negotiating and posturing, resolutions had been made and dates had been set, nothing seemed to be happening. Gladys and R.G. begged Cindy not to go. To them, any place in the Middle East was inherently unsafe. But Cindy wanted to go home. She couldn't stay in Mocksville forever. She missed Mohammed. She missed Khorfakkan. Mocksville was home, but so was Khorfakkan, and it was time to go. The danger was not in Khorfakkan, it was being in the air. If something happened while they were in the air, and flights were delayed, diverted, or canceled, they could end up stranded somewhere.

"Look," she told them. "We're just as safe there as we are here. Nothing is going to happen to us in the UAE. We'll be safe there. Don't worry!"

Cindy flew home to Khorfakkan in November. By early January, 1991, negotiations had turned sour. The United States was worried that Iraq would attack its closest neighbor, Saudi Arabia, to gain control of the bulk of the world's oil supply. And there were stories of human rights abuses in Iraq. The United States was threatening to intervene. The United Nations Security Council set a deadline, demanding that Iraq withdraw from Kuwait by January 15th.

That first week in January Randy called, begging Cindy to come home. It was looking more and more like there would be a war, and the whole family, everybody, was worried. They wanted her to come home where, in their eyes, she would be safe.

"Look, I'm not coming home. I'm safe here." Cindy said. "I just came back. Even if I wanted to come back, we can't afford it. I'm not coming home. There's nothing going to happen to me here." They didn't understand that Khorfakkan was a tiny, unimportant seaside village compared to Abu Dhabi, Dubai, or even the Port of Fujairah. She was far away from Iraq and Kuwait. She was safe.

But they were desperate for her to come home. R.G. offered to pay. He'd borrow money if he had to. No, she insisted. She was staying put.

"I feel fine here," she said. "It's fine."

On January 13th, the family called again. First it was Gladys on the phone, but before she could speak she began to cry.

Wow. They are really scared for me, Cindy thought. Then Randy got on the phone.

"I have some bad news," he said quietly. "Dad was in a car accident today. He – he's gone." He waited a moment and then said, "Are you coming home?"

"You're lying to me. Nothing's happened to him. You're just trying to get me to come home."

"No. Look, I wouldn't do that to you."

It couldn't be true. It wasn't true. *It can't be true.*

But in her gut, she knew that it wasn't like Randy to make something like that up. He wouldn't do that to her. Of all the brothers, he was the one who was always her protector, never her tormentor. It wasn't like him. It wasn't like any of them. But it couldn't be true. Just couldn't.

But it was. R.G. had been driving home from work when he came up behind a state trooper's car with its lights flashing. Thinking that the police were pulling someone over, R.G. changed lanes to pass and drove straight into the path of a drunk driver who was going in the wrong direction on the freeway. As the police watched, helpless to stop him, R.G. and the other car collided head-on. R.G. was killed instantly.

How could she get home? Was it even possible? Cindy's oldest brother Terry got in touch with the Red Cross, and then the embassy called. "If you want to go, we'll get you home," they said. There were no commercial flights; they'd all been canceled. She would have to get a military flight.

Cindy was in anguish. The Middle East was in a state of emergency – Mohammed wasn't coming home any time soon. She had two babies. She'd just been home. How could she go back? Her father was dead, and her mother was alone now. How could she not go back? She didn't know what to do.

More than anything, Cindy wanted to be there for her mother. Gladys was worried about Cindy but now Cindy was equally worried about Gladys. "She's all alone over there," Gladys was telling people. But no, she wasn't, Cindy told her mother, told them all. Cindy had people in her house all the time, supporting and consoling her. The house was never empty. But Gladys didn't understand that, and now she needed Cindy, and Cindy didn't want to let her mother down.

Mohammed was begging her, please, do not go. "If you stay here, I promise you as soon as this is over, you can go and stay as long as you want," he pleaded. "Right now, it's very difficult. It is too dangerous to fly. I don't want you to go."

Mohammed's wishes were clear, but it was still her decision to make. An impossible decision, but one that had to be made. Their world was on the brink of war. As bad as it was to be apart from Mohammed when he might go to war any day now, it would be even worse to leave her daughters, and if she went she would have to leave them behind. She could not expose them to the risk. So, she made her decision. She didn't go.

Roy Gattis Davis was buried on January 17, 1991, with the bulk of Davie County in attendance. He was sixty years old. That same day, the air campaign known as Operation Desert Storm was launched. The Gulf War had begun.

The next day, in addition to a story about the funeral services, the Davie County Enterprise Record ran a story with the headline: FATHER DIES, DAUGHTER TRAPPED IN MIDDLE EAST. When Cindy heard about the story she thought: *They make it sound like I'm a prisoner here.* Everybody back home always thought that anything that happened in the Middle East was happening directly to her.

The war lasted until the end of February, when the Iraqi forces withdrew from Kuwait. *Hamdullah*, Mohammed was not sent into combat. Nevertheless, the war had a direct impact on Khorfakkan. As they retreated, the Iraqi military set fire to seven hundred oil wells, fires that burned for almost two years. The smoke and soot from the fires drifted south into the UAE. Whenever it rained in Khorfakkan, the water ran black in the streets, making oily puddles. There was no water from God for people to gather, and there wouldn't be for a very long time. Nobody drank it. Nobody cleansed with it. The water from Heaven had been spoiled by war.

That April, Cindy went back home to Mocksville and, as Mohammed had promised, she stayed with Gladys as long as she wanted. That summer was a hot one, with lots of thunderstorms. One day as the girls were napping, she and her mother sat sipping sweet tea on the screened porch as they watched a storm approach. Cindy jumped up.

"Where y'all going now?"

"Just a minute," Cindy said. She ran into the kitchen and fetched the biggest, widest bowl she could find. Setting it in the middle of the table out on the patio where it could catch the rain she said, "We're going to get us some water from Heaven. It's what Muslim people do at home in Khorfakkan."

The storm hit with a crack, and then a wallop. Lightning and thunder was followed by wind, and then the rain came. It rained so hard they couldn't even see the bowl out there. It felt like every heartache, every joy, every loss, everything in her bittersweet life, was washing down to her from above. She thought of her father who had begged her to come home the week before he died. She didn't get to say goodbye. She thought of Abdulrahman, who left behind his two daughters and newborn baby boy. She thought of Moza the sweet banana lady, and all the young cousins of Mohammed's that had been killed on the roads. She thought of her cousin's only child, a daughter, killed in a car crash at age sixteen. She'd missed that funeral, too. She thought of the worry and pain she'd caused Gladys when she married Mohammed. She wished she could do more to make up for it now that R.G. was gone and Gladys was alone.

The rain stopped. The skies cleared. Cindy went out to fetch the bowl. It was overflowing. It had caught more water than seemed possible. "Here, Mama," she said. "This is water from Heaven, where Daddy is right now. God sent it from Heaven to show us that Daddy is up there with Him." They drank some, and Cindy took the rest into her room. That evening at sundown, she washed with the water from Heaven, and then prayed that the years that were taken from her father be added to the life of her mother.

Chapter 11: Abu Dhabi Decision

1992

Cindy was tired of living in one room. It had been ten years since they married. Mohammed's house was her house but it was also his mother house, and his father's. His children from the marriage to Aisha were grown up, and yet there they were, still in the house. She was tired of living with all the in-laws and stepchildren. He had bought the bigger house; he had paid for it. But here she was, still living in this room. So, what had she gained? What had he done for her?

Their two girls were getting bigger. They had toys that Cindy couldn't leave outside. She had to bring them in each night and put them in the bedroom where they slept, or they would be broken by the other kids in the neighborhood. No matter what she said or did, the neighborhood kids could not keep their hands off. They didn't understand the idea that something belonged to someone else. So, everything had to come inside. Into her room.

Happiness wasn't something that just happened. You had to make it with what you had. Cindy was good at that. Whereas other people would have complained, she always looked at it from the other direction. She might not have everything that other people had, but it didn't matter. Mohammed would always do anything he could to make her happy. And the things he couldn't do? Well, how could she complain about that? He was doing his best. But this living with everybody was getting to be too much.

When Mohammed came home for the weekend, Cindy broached the subject by offering him an idea. If they had to stay in that house, they should build another room so that she and the children would have more space. Other people built new rooms onto their houses all the time. When she suggested the idea Mohammed, as always, consulted his family.

And oh! The uproar!

"No! You cannot build another room!" Ali Mubarak shouted. "Do not build anything!"

Mohammed told Cindy, "My father won't allow it."

"Then why the hell'd you ask him?" Cindy exploded. "It's *your house!* But no, no, no, *he* doesn't *agree* to it?" Her voice rose in pitch, and the words came tumbling out on top of each other. "I don't care that he doesn't agree! Listen to me. This is YOUR HOUSE! You can do what you want to do! You bought it. You paid for it. It's in YOUR NAME. Why do you even care what he thinks? He should be grateful to be living here!"

"Yes, this is true. You are right." Mohammed began. "But –"

But Cindy was just getting started. "Look around you!" she cried. "How many Arab wives do you see who are living with their in-laws after ten years? You try and find me one local lady who would live with her mother-in-law after ten years! You're not going to find it."

She had a point. All marriages began with a marriage contract, and these days most brides stipulated that they would not live with the mother-in-law. When Cindy and Mohammed were married, it was still normal for a new wife to live with the in-laws for the first year. But not for ten.

"Honey," Mohammed pleaded. "Please. Just let it go. For the sake of my sanity. He has his reasons. Just drop it." Mohammed had reasons, too, for consulting his family, even if Cindy didn't completely understand them. He consulted them on everything. And they still thought that Cindy controlled Mohammed, that he did anything she said. They accused Mohammed of not having a mind of his own.

"He does whatever *she* tells him to do," Zamzam was fond of saying. They were comparing Cindy to how a local lady would act and they'd forgotten what she had given up to be with him. He should be trying to make her happy. They had no idea how patient she'd been. Zamzam wanted Mohammed to get rid of Cindy. To get an Emirati wife. She told anyone who would listen, "If she were a daughter of the country, she wouldn't be doing that."

If I were a local lady, honey, Cindy thought, *I wouldn't be living in your house for ten years!*

She was tired of listening to Zamzam tell people that Mohammed had plucked her out of poverty and she should be grateful for everything he did. As if she were a refugee. "When she first came here," Zamzam told people, "she was skinny. She was so hungry she ate a whole chicken every day. Now, she is fat." The truth was, between them all, a chicken had lasted four days back then. She hadn't gained any weight until she was in the United States, and had Aminah. She had gained, but it was from the babies.

"Ok, then. Fine." Cindy said. But something had snapped. "If you're not going to build any rooms, then you get me out of this house. I don't have enough room. Besides, we don't need to be sleeping with the kids. They're too big. You just rent me an apartment." There were some nice spacious apartments in town, and she knew that they could get into one.

"No!" Mohammed protested. "This is my home town! You don't rent an apartment in your home town. We have a house. You live at home."

No matter what, she was not going to live in that crowded house any longer. "All right, then – I want to move to Abu Dhabi."

That had always been the deal. When Mohammed got caught up on the money, they would move to Abu Dhabi. He had paid off the divorce. Then he'd bought another house. Then he'd gotten into a bad business deal with a friend, and had to pay the debt that his friend left. The base where Mohammed had worked when they were first married had moved off the island, and was now part of Zayed Military City, south of Abu Dhabi. If Cindy moved there, the military would rent them an apartment and the 2,000-dirham monthly housing allowance would be deducted from Mohammed's paycheck. That was money he had needed to pay his debts. But he'd been promoted, and his salary had increased. They could move to Abu Dhabi now. They could afford it.

To Emiratis, Khorfakkan was a place to get out of. Compared to Dubai or Abu Dhabi, there was nothing there. People scoffed whenever Khorfakkan was mentioned. It was a nothing place. Dubai was the place to be, where everything was happening. Abu Dhabi was smaller, more conservative – backwards, some said. But compared to Khorfakkan – well, there was no comparison.

Abu Dhabi city was on Abu Dhabi island, an oblong sand bar jutting out into the Persian Gulf and separated from the mainland by a narrow waterway called Khor Al Maqta. The original village, a cluster of huts with streets of trodden sand, was long gone, replaced by the city's first fort, school, and houses. When Cindy saw Abu Dhabi that first weekend, dropping Mohammed off at the base on the outskirts of the city, she had seen an expanse of sand before her, the growing city skyline rising in the distance to the north. Now wide paved roads divided the featureless salt plain into long city blocks, stretching on out to the bleak outskirts of the city, waiting to be built out. Sheikh Zayed had called in modernist planners and architects, and the result was a city that could easily have been transplanted into any post-World War II landscape. High rise concrete towers, balconied apartment buildings, and monumental government and administrative complexes dominated the skyline. Shopping centers were under construction in every block. Westerners were streaming in to fill jobs in the finance, business consulting, and management sectors, living in hotels as they waited for permanent housing to be completed. Indian and Pakistani workers were coming by the planeload to work construction jobs.

Abu Dhabi was famous for its stretch of beach along its Corniche. Cindy rarely went to the beach in Khorfakkan. She covered, so why bother? When she was growing up in North Carolina, the Davises went to the mountains, not the beach. She loved the mountains and the sea breeze in Khorfakkan. It was cooler there than in Abu Dhabi. She liked small-town life in Khorfakkan. It was like Mocksville, in some ways. At home, people would say, "The best thing about living in a small town is when you don't know what you're doing, someone else does." The same was true in Khorfakkan. After ten years, Khorfakkan was home. Annoying as Mohammed's family sometimes was, they were there if she needed them, they were her family now, and they needed her, too.

Cindy had always longed to be closer to Mohammed. Those first years as a newlywed, separated during the week, had been crushingly lonely. If they hadn't gone to El Paso and Denver where they could live together like a normal couple, she wasn't sure what she would have done. It was always the promise of Abu Dhabi, having her own place, being together, that had kept her strong. But now she had mixed feelings.

Almost every evening, Cindy walked over to Auntie Aminah's house to sit with her and a couple of the neighbors, drink tea, and talk about whatever topic came up. Aminah was Mohammed's cousin, but being closer to Zamzam's age than to Mohammed's she was considered an auntie. One evening, the topic of the move to Abu Dhabi came up.

"You will not be able to visit." Everyone was glum. "Why you go to Abu Dhabi?" they said. "Don't leave! Stay here!" It reminded Cindy of people in Mocksville when she was on the brink of marrying Mohammed. But this time was different. Instead of dropping everything to be with him, she was worried that she would regret it.

"I don't really want to go," she heard herself admitting. "But if I stay here, I don't get my own place. Mohammed wants me to stay in the house and live in that room, and I don't want to. I want my own place. I can't live in that house any longer."

Cindy had always thought she wanted to live together with Mohammed, but now she had to admit something, if only to herself. She and Mohammed had been living apart during the week for ten years, and it had worked out well. She could do whatever she wanted during the week, whenever. She could eat when she wanted, go to bed when she wanted. She could stay up all night reading, watching TV, or listening to music. What if she packed up her life, moved to Abu Dhabi, and then – and then they didn't get along as well?

"Mohammed is against me getting my own place," Cindy told the ladies. "He says if I want to live in Khorfakkan, we already have a house. I would rather move to Abu Dhabi than live in one room for the rest of my life!"

"Why does he want to take you away from us?" Aminah exclaimed. "You don't have any family here, and we cannot help you if you ever need it there. Let me talk to him. I will convince him to let you stay in Khorfakkan and get your own place, *inshallah.*"

The next weekend when Mohammed came home, they went to visit Auntie Aminah, and she really let him have it.

"Why you take Sindiya to Abu Dhabi?" she demanded. "Leave her here with us! What if something happens? Who takes care of her? Here, we take care of her!"

Mohammed was cornered. Above all, he wanted Cindy to be happy. She wouldn't stay in the house any longer, but she wasn't excited to move to Abu Dhabi. The only other solution, until they could get another house, was to rent an apartment. An apartment in his own home town, for the love of God.

Auntie Aminah wasn't finished yet. "What is wrong with renting a place for Sindiya in Khorfakkan? Everyone rents these days! No one lives with their in-laws for more than a year or two anymore!"

Walking home, Mohammed said, "So, do you want to go to Abu Dhabi with me, or do you want to rent an apartment here in Khorfakkan?"

"I'd like to stay here," Cindy said. It wasn't only her and Mohammed to consider any more, it was their daughters. Aminah was in kindergarten. "When I told Aminah that we were moving, she cried and said, 'I don't want to go to another school! I like my school, and I like my teacher!' I don't want to move away from all my friends that I've made here in Khorfakkan and start all over again."

To her surprise, relief flooded Cindy, turning her face pink. She thought for a moment that she might burst into tears. She hadn't known, until that moment, how much she had dreaded moving to Abu Dhabi. How different she was from the blushing bride who had boarded that plane ten years before.

"Ok," Mohammed said. "*Inshallah,* we'll find you a place here."

Cindy was thirty years old with two little girls, moving into her own place for the first time in her life. It was her tenth anniversary gift. They found a spacious apartment with seven rooms – a living room, dining room, kitchen, four bedrooms, and two bathrooms, one in the master bedroom and one for the rest of the house. The rent was 1,000 dirhams per month – half of what it would have been in Abu Dhabi.

Since it wasn't within walking distance of Mohammed's house, she could choose when to see her mother-in-law. She relished the privacy, alone during the weekdays and with Mohammed on the weekends.

Without Zamzam's housemaid in the kitchen, she could cook anything she pleased. Tuna and rice casserole, fried chicken and biscuits, pot pie, mashed potatoes and gravy, lasagna. Although Mohammed liked American food – he was particularly fond of her macaroni and cheese – he always wanted rice when he was home. Arabs had rice with every meal. "If I don't eat rice," he always said, "I haven't eaten!"

Mohammed wanted her to get a housemaid, but Cindy resisted. Everyone else had help, but she was determined never to bring in a housemaid, even with the large apartment. She'd seen too many people have problems with them.

The UAE had strict rules about who could come into the country, and under what circumstances. Any foreigner applying for a resident visa had to have a sponsor – a spouse who was an Emirati national, like Mohammed, or an employer. Wives and families of expats could be sponsored by the husband. Laborers almost never brought their families with them – they lived in all-male workers' camps, or overcrowded apartments. There were two ways to hire a maid. You could sponsor one from India, Pakistan, Bangladesh, or North Africa, or you could go through an agency. You never knew what you were getting, but usually it was a young girl who knew nothing and you would have to train her. She would have to learn how to cook, clean, and do laundry. Some girls were there to try to find a husband, and they would always want to go out with the family, as if she were one of the children or a sister, not the housekeeper. If you sponsored a housemaid, it was a three-year contract. If it didn't work out, you were stuck with her for three long years.

"You need someone with you," Mohammed said. "You shouldn't be there by yourself at night." She'd had been living under the same roof with his family for ten years, and the idea of her being on her own, without someone else at night, worried him.

Cindy flatly rejected the idea. "I don't want a housemaid," she said. "I don't need anyone here with me. This is Khorfakkan, not New York City." It wasn't worth the trouble. She was American, and she knew how to keep a house cleaner than any maid. She would be fine at night. It would be a relief to be on her own, out of Zamzam's watchful gaze for the first time.

It didn't matter that she didn't have a maid living with her; Cindy was never alone in that building. One of the reasons they'd chosen it was because one of Mohammed's cousins lived there. Cindy knew Yasmeen well – they'd met within days of when Cindy had arrived in Khorfakkan – and both husbands worked in Abu Dhabi, leaving their wives during the week. Cindy soon found out that there were other neighbors in the building whose husbands worked in Abu Dhabi. It was a common theme, the wife living in an apartment while the husband worked away during the week. During the summer, when it was too hot to go out during the day, they often lingered in each other's apartments until two or three in the morning, enjoying the cool breezes wafting through the open windows and talking as their children slept nearby. It wasn't acceptable for ladies to be out late at night, but they were in the privacy of their own apartment building, so it didn't matter. It was like a sorority house. But with children.

Weekends were two days now, Thursday and Friday. Thursday was like Saturday in the United States, and Friday was a day for prayer, like Sunday for Christians. Mohammed and Cindy spent their Thursdays in Khorfakkan doing errands and taking the kids to a shopping center with an indoor play area when it was too hot for them to play outside. On Fridays, they usually went out for lunch. It was a treat to be able to go out without Zamzam's constant presence. It was the same with their occasional trips to Dubai. They never let her know they were going until they were already half way there – then Mohammed would use his cell phone to call and break the news. Zamzam was always angry at being left behind and when they got home, she stomped around the house banging and slamming any object within reach – a cup, a teapot, her handbag, a door – earning her the nickname "Bambam." Then, eventually, she got over it.

On Fridays, they went to Mohammed's Uncle Abdulrahman's, where Cindy could expect the uncle's wife, Umm Ishab, to bring up the subject of children. "Umm Aminah," Umm Ishab said each time she saw Cindy. "*Inshallah,* you should get pregnant again. Have a son, *inshallah.*"

"If God had meant for me to have a son," Cindy always replied, "He had two chances to give me one."

She and Mohammed had agreed that two was enough. It was one of the ways that, as a couple, they were more American than Emirati. Large families were increasingly rare in the United States, but Emiratis were expected to have as many children as possible, to build the Emirati population which was far outnumbered by foreign nationals. Sons were especially desirable. Every Emirati family needed as many sons as possible. Mohammed had three sons from his first marriage, but everyone thought that he should have a son with Cindy. Everyone, that is, except Cindy and Mohammed.

"If you had a son, what would you name him?" Umm Ishab asked one Friday.

"Oh, I don't know. Maybe Faisal, or Sultan."

"Umm Faisal! It is a good name. That is your name now," Umm Ishab said with satisfaction. Then, raising her hands in the air, she prayed for Cindy's birth control to fail. "Allah, give Umm Faisal a son."

Within a few weeks, Cindy knew she was pregnant. Aminah was eight, Aisha was five, and thanks to Umm Ishab and her prayer, Cindy was having another baby. "I'd like a boy," she told people when they asked. "I have an Emirati girl and an American girl. I want a boy who is Emirati and American – half and half." Of course, his name would be Faisal.

As soon as the news got out, the gifts began pouring in from the new friends Cindy had made – not just the neighbors, but their sisters, in-laws, cousins. Whenever there was a wedding, a birth, or a death, Cindy had paid a visit to congratulate the family or offer her condolences, and this endeared her to the community. To her great surprise, she received not only baby gifts but gold trinkets, necklaces and rings, a symbol of her value to the giver.

Cindy enjoyed doing her own cleaning. Compared to the neighbors', her house was spotless. *These people,* she thought, *don't know how to clean.* They'd been living in dust for so long, they didn't even see it. They had housemaids and still they had roaches. When she was seven months' pregnant, heavy and exhausted, they found that the neighbors' roaches had moved in. Mohammed put his foot down.

"For the love of God, Cindy, you have got to get help!" he insisted. Cindy relented, and agreed to take on a part-time maid through an agency, just for a few hours each morning to help with the cleaning and stay with baby Faisal, after he was born, while she took the girls to school. Cindy still cooked her own lunch and did most of the housework, determined not to rely on a housemaid.

The baby was overdue, and it was decided to induce labor. Cindy was admitted to the hospital, accompanied by Mohammed. Half the neighborhood, including Umm Ishab, came to visit and were present in the room when Cindy's water broke. Her labor began and as she breathed through a contraction, Cindy heard Umm Ishab, who did not approve of inducing labor, comment, "Next time she waits for the baby. It comes when God wills it."

This is all her fault! Cindy thought. *Umm Ishab, you did this!* As the contraction crested, then subsided, Cindy shouted at the top of her lungs, "THERE WILL BE NO NEXT TIME!" The baby was coming. The nurse ushered everyone out except Mohammed. Cindy was wheeled into the delivery room. Even though it was against hospital rules, Mohammed was allowed to stay with his American wife for the birth. For Cindy and Mohammed, rules were always flexible. The baby came, a beautiful, peaceful boy, with a complexion that was neither dark nor light – it was half and half. They named him Faisal.

"You always get what you wish for, don't you, Umm Faisal?" people said.

One weekend soon afterward Mohammed brought a surprise home. "There was an auction at work," he said, lugging in a computer. "I don't want it, but I think you might like it." Cindy didn't know anything about computers, but it made no difference. Mohammed knew she was smart. She could figure it out. He'd put in a bid, and won.

Cindy fell in love with the computer. After the kids were in bed, she would turn it on and start pressing buttons. The military had removed all files from the memory, leaving programs and games installed. She spent hours playing Tetris and Lemmings, and tinkering with word processing, spreadsheets, the calculator. Discovering.

Living in the apartment free of Zamzam was a blessing that didn't last forever. When Cindy had been in the apartment for a year, Zamzam persuaded Mohammed that she was too far away. She wanted them nearer. "There is a house for rent! Come rent this house!" she pestered Mohammed. "Rent this house! Rent this house! *Rent this house!*" To pacify her, Mohammed signed a lease for the house that Zamzam had picked out. Cindy was not happy about moving, but she went along with it to keep peace in the family. When she moved into the apartment, they'd had to buy all the furnishings new, as well as appliances. Now everything had to be moved and stored at the new house for the summer. Cindy was taking the three children home to North Carolina, where she could escape the soaring temperatures in the UAE. When she returned, they would move in.

Summer in North Carolina was a slice of heaven. The family welcomed Cindy with a big party, and everybody made a fuss over the new baby. Gladys spoiled her granddaughters with frilly dresses, dolls, and anything else she could find that was girly. She doted on Faisal, exclaiming that he was such a good baby. Aminah was quiet but Aisha, who was indeed the spitting image of her Uncle Randy, was a tomboy. Cindy's childhood home was on a large piece of property at the end of a dead-end road with an expanse of lawn, a grove of trees, and a woodland next door. Aisha played outside all day, running with her boy cousins. If they were in Khorfakkan, she would have to stay inside. It would be too hot to play. Yes, it was heaven to be home in summer, instead of in the hot, dry Middle East. She loved watching the clouds gathering in the mountains. It was heaven when it rained.

I have the best of both worlds, Cindy realized. She loved her adopted country and her life with Mohammed, and she could still come back to Mocksville and be with her American family. Every weekend throughout the summer, the whole family gathered after morning church and had Sunday dinner.

Cindy went to the Baptist church, and people there knew she was Muslim. They were curious about her life. "Do you have to cover your face over there?" "Do you wear a *burka*?" "Can you go out?" Thanks to magazines like *LIFE* and *National Geographic,* which had run stories about women in Saudi Arabia and Afghanistan, most people thought that all women in the Middle East lived very restrictive lives and were made to cover from head to toe with only a tiny panel to see out of. They assumed that she wasn't allowed to drive, and that she had to ask permission from her husband to go anywhere. They didn't realize that she probably had more freedom from her husband than they had from theirs.

"No," Cindy answered. "The UAE isn't like that. People don't wear *burkas* where I live."

Women wore burkas in Afghanistan, India, and Pakistan. Some of the Bedouin women in Khorfakkan and nearby Oman wore a traditional mask, embellished with gold trim, called *burqa,* or "beauty mask," as a sign of the beauty of womanhood. Cindy had seen it on that very first day when she sat with the ladies while Mohammed's brother Abdulrahman had translated. She had tried one on. But would this distinction, she wondered, be lost on her hometown friends and neighbors? She decided to keep it as simple as possible.

"Some of them wear a *niqab*, but that's different," she explained. "It's more like a cloth over their face. But I don't wear one. People wear it if they want to, usually because they're more religious." That last part was mostly true. Sometimes the husband or bothers insisted and in those cases, it was about control. Cindy had an Emirati friend whose husband had insisted she wear the *niqab* when they went on a trip to Australia. People had stared at her. She was embarrassed.

"I wear a black cloak called an *abaya* when I go out, and a matching scarf called a *shayla,* on my head," Cindy said. "It's the Emirati national dress." Over the years, as the UAE had developed a national identity, the men's signature *kandura* style, subtly different from that of other Arab countries, had emerged as the national dress for men, and the black *abaya* and *shayla* for women. No longer merely a symbol of religiosity, the women's garments were now a symbol of nationalism and pride. But it was one of those things that Westerners had trouble grasping. To them, any woman who covered must be oppressed. To an Emirati woman, it was just the opposite. Why should they be expected to show their body to anyone who wanted to look?

"What do you with your time?" "Do y'all ever go out places together?" "Do y'all have parties like here?" Cindy tried to explain how it was the same, people over there were the same in many ways. But it was different. Some things were different. An Emirati woman over the age of eighteen could own land, but very few did. They could have their own bank accounts. Women owned businesses. Yet it was a society guided by Sharia law, giving men power. It was deeply embedded in their culture, if not the law, that a woman could not live alone, could not travel alone, and should not interact with men to whom she was not related. A wife needed a letter of permission to obtain a driver's license, or to cross the border into another country. When Cindy traveled, Mohammed went to the agent and booked the ticket for her – it was easier that way. Men made all the major decisions and purchases, and often shopped with or for their wives for even the most mundane household items. Cindy had more freedom than most, because she was American. And she was married to Mohammed.

Cindy thought her life in the UAE wasn't much more restricted than it would have been if she'd stayed and married a local boy. The UAE wasn't the only place where men wielded power over women; the United States could be chauvinistic too. When did women gain the right to vote in the United States? Not until 1920. The Equal Rights Amendment, which had been introduced in 1923 and remained controversial for the past seventy years, had not been ratified. How many women owned businesses? Ran companies? Why didn't the United States have more women in political office? Would they ever have a woman President? It was all a matter of degrees, and considering that the UAE had been a country for less than thirty years, they had done well. Women could vote there, and they were attending universities in Al Ain, Abu Dhabi, and Dubai. They owned businesses and held high-paying government jobs. It was Sheikh Zayed's vision that all Emirati citizens, both men and women, be educated – albeit in separate institutions – and it was paid for by the government.

Their real differences were in their social patterns. Men and women socialized completely separately in the UAE, with the women in one room and men in the other. At meals, men and women were served separately, and ate in separate rooms. Weddings were completely segregated affairs with women and men celebrating side-by-side in separate but identical wedding halls or tents. When Cindy explained some of these customs, people gasped. It all sounded quite extreme, but when you lived there, it was normal. It was fine. Cindy enjoyed the company of the Emirati ladies, just as she enjoyed the company of American women of Mocksville when they had their ladies' get-togethers. The only thing different was the weddings and parties.

People who criticized weren't thinking about the fact that men and women gathered separately everywhere. There were so many men-only and women-only organizations in Mocksville alone, she couldn't count them. Look at the American men who all but lived in their garages with their televisions, watching sports. How was that so different from Mohammed going out at night to sit in the *majlis* with his friends? It was tradition; it was their culture. But it wasn't the law. When they had expat friends over to visit, there was no rule that said they could not invite the husbands and wives to dine with the family. If Cindy's family ever came to visit, they would behave like a normal American family.

But so far, as much as she asked them to, no one in her family had made the trip. It had been over ten years, and they didn't understand her life, because they hadn't gone to the UAE to see it for themselves.

When it was time to leave, they threw a huge party. The whole town turned out, it seemed, and there were piles of gifts for her and the kids, tons of food, and a huge goodbye cake. Cindy's heart – and her luggage – were full, but she was worried about what might happen the next time they came to visit. She had an American passport, but the kids were Emirati, and they had Emirati passports. When they entered the country, the U.S. Immigration and Customs officials had questioned her.

"You're their mother? Then they are American. They should have U.S. passports, not visas."

"They can't have two passports," Cindy had explained. "It's against the law in the UAE. They can't have dual citizenship. They'd have to give up their Emirati citizenship." They had let them in, but she didn't want to go through that again. Perhaps she could get a long-term visa. The problem was, they didn't easily fit into any of the categories. She and Mohammed had agreed that they would alternate her summer trips home with other trips – she looked forward to seeing Paris the next summer. So, for now, it didn't matter. There was time to figure it out, *inshallah.*

Chapter 12: *Djïnn* and Black Magic

1995

Cindy's luggage was packed with toys, movies, and gifts from America. This time, she'd brought a couple of empty suitcases to hold everything. They were bursting at the seams with Disney Princesses, Power Puff Girls, Beanie Babies, Littlest Pet Shop, play telephones, and any other toy that was new and popular that year. Faisal had fallen in love with American baseball, and he kept a bat and ball under his pillow at night. Scattered among all the suitcases, tucked in with the clothing, toys, and sundries that she couldn't get in the UAE, were the movies. The UAE never had the latest movies that were out on VCR; it took months or years before they would be shown on the cable television station, and it was virtually impossible to buy anything American on VCR. The video tapes in the stores were all Bollywood movies and Japanese anime.

Cindy had learned not to pack all the movies together in one suitcase. The UAE had strict decency laws, and it was illegal to bring in anything containing nudity. When she had brought in a stack of tapes that she'd recorded off the television and packed together in one suitcase, customs had found and taken them.

"What is this?" the customs official had asked.

"Video tapes. Movies."

"Is it pornography? It is illegal."

"No, of course it's not pornography." But she couldn't prove it. There were no labels, no trademarks. There was no way to prove that they were children's movies. So, to be safe, they had taken them.

This time, she'd packed more carefully, buying the videos and distributing them among their five suitcases. For the kids, she brought both *An American Tail* movies, *The Brave Little Toaster*, *The Rescuers*, and *Beauty and the Beast*. She also had movies for Hassan, who loved horror: *Body Parts, Dead Again, Cape Fear,* and *Black Magic* – it was set in North Carolina.

She wished that she could have brought *Aladdin,* but it wasn't coming out on video until later that year. Gladys promised to send it as soon as it came out. The hit Disney movie had popularized the story in *1001 Arabian Nights* about the boy, the princess, and the *djinni* in the bottle. Forever after, Americans would associate the word "genie" with a benevolent spirit in a bottle and a magic carpet that flew.

People in Khorfakkan firmly believed in the shape-shifting *djinn* who they said roamed the uninhabited places surrounding them, bestowing benefits or wreaking havoc as they saw fit. They also believed in the darker art of black magic. Officially, black magic was against the law, but under certain circumstances, such as when a malevolent *djinni* came to inhabit a human and caused her to do evil, it was permitted. Just before she'd left for her summer in North Carolina, Cindy had seen it.

One of the neighbors in the apartment building had a teenaged daughter. She was a good girl, who suddenly began doing wicked things. She behaved disrespectfully. She smoked cigarettes. The family, convinced that she was possessed, summoned the *imam* from the mosque to do an exorcism. Standing over the girl's bed for several hours as her family and neighbors looked on in support, the *imam* read verses and parables from the Quran asking God's help to drive out the demon. When the reading was finished, the *imam* spoke directly to the *djinni.*

"Why are you hurting this girl?" he asked. "What has she done to you? Has she stepped upon you, or one of yours? Did she pour boiling water upon you, or your daughter? Have you had your revenge? Have you done enough harm?" Then he gave the girl pure holy water to drink, released an acrid smoke above her, and called for the evil spirit to vanish as she fell asleep. The next morning, the girl's sweet nature had been restored.

Cindy was thinking of the apartment, her neighbors, and the teenage girl as she arrived at the rental house. She would miss living in the apartment, and she didn't relish the idea of starting over, setting up a household again. It was dusk on Saturday, Mohammed had gone back to the military base, and she was managing all three children while trying to turn on the lights. Suddenly baby Faisal, who was usually quiet and complacent, erupted in a fit of screaming. Realizing that the electricity was off, Cindy found the fuse box and turned on the lights as Faisal continued to wail, despite her attempts at soothing. Looking around, she could see that the house was dismal and dirty. Disgusted, she thought to herself, *Oh, man. Look how much work I'm going to have to do.* They would have to live with Zamzam until she could get the house ready. She would have to thoroughly clean it, set up the kitchen, and move all their furniture and belongings in. There was barely enough time to get it all done before school started.

It was an older house, but big. Too big, really. The front passageway connected an oversized *majlis* to a large main kitchen and a couple of small utility rooms, probably intended as storage and maid's quarters. The area that Cindy could imagine as their living quarters was behind the big kitchen; several nondescript rooms were clustered together in the back of the property with small passageways between them. Another larger passageway divided the front from the back rooms. Everything was surrounded by a seven-foot concrete wall with an iron gate at the front entrance and several side gates around the periphery, all of which locked. It seemed like the house had been built in phases without a plan or design. It was – well, cattywampus. Cindy was beginning to understand Ali Mubarak's reluctance to add onto their house. Looking around, she realized he'd probably been right. But she was too stubborn to admit it, even to Mohammed.

"I don't know about this house," she said to Mohammed when they talked on the phone. "The living room is too big. I'm going to use it for storage. And I'm not eating out of that kitchen. It creeps me out."

"It creeps you out?" Mohammed repeated.

"Yes, it's too far away from the rest of the house. I'm going to use the rooms in the back. This place just doesn't make sense."

She set up her kitchen first, putting the cooking stove in a room next to a smaller room with a sink. Another room would be their living room, and there was one bedroom for the two girls and one for her and Mohammed, when he was home, to sleep with the baby. She left the other extra rooms empty.

They moved in as school was about to start. The evening before the first day of school, Cindy put Aminah and Aisha to bed telling them "Now, don't you get up." But soon they remembered that they wanted their Disney backpacks, which were out in the *majlis*. Cindy waited until she thought they were asleep, and then ventured out to the big room where everything that hadn't yet been unpacked was stored.

As she searched through the piles, Cindy heard familiar footsteps. *Ch-ch-ch-ch* ...! She knew those naughty footsteps. They were Aisha's, the one who didn't listen. Exasperated, she sighed. *I told her, don't get up.* Cindy went back and checked their room, but they were, both sound asleep in bed. She shook off the creepy feeling and didn't think about it again.

As the days blended into weeks, Cindy felt a change come over her. In the evenings, after the kids were put to bed, she'd get an eerie feeling. She was uneasy being there alone during the week, a feeling she'd never had before. She felt short-tempered all the time. It wasn't like her, to be in a bad mood for no reason. She'd never been an angry parent with the kids. Normally, if they spilled or dropped something, or left their toys out, she just told them to clean it up. Both she and Mohammed would laugh at their silly antics. But in that house, if something happened – POW! Aisha was little, but not too little to remember later the change in her mother. She'd turned dark. She was blaming them for things they didn't do. Cindy saw it, the change in herself, but she couldn't control it. Something small would happen, and she became enraged.

One evening when they'd been in the house a month, the kids were asleep and Cindy was alone in the living room watching television when she heard a door handle jiggle. At first, she thought it was the neighbor's son Ahmed, who was born with a mild mental handicap. Ahmed sometimes wandered into their house, which Cindy didn't mind. She got up to check. But then, wait a minute. She remembered that she'd locked all the outside gates, and all the doors to the house were locked as well. How could he get in? He couldn't.

Instead of going outside to look, Cindy decided to call Mohmmed's son Jassim, who was living with Zamzam. "There's somebody trying to get into my house. Can you come over and check it out?"

Moments later, the whole family was at her gate – Zamzam, Ali, and the three stepsons. When Cindy opened the gate, there was a flurry of sound and a blur of activity above their heads. She jumped back, and they all saw a black shape, the shape of a cat, suspended in mid-air. Then it was gone.

Cindy hadn't seen it well, but she thought – *Big deal. It's a cat.* She liked cats; they were everywhere. People had them as pets, and feral cats roamed the streets, raiding garbage cans and sleeping during the day in any cool shady place they could find. She wasn't going to let this scare her. But it still made her a little uneasy.

Strange sounds became a regular nighttime pattern. Odd little things were happening. One day, while she was hanging laundry outside behind the family room, Cindy heard a noisy thump followed by Faisal's screams. *Oh, God,* she thought, *what did Aisha do to him now?* Running into the house to where she'd thought she'd heard the noise, she found the living room empty. Surely, she'd heard it. A mother knows her own child's scream. But none of them were there. Looking outside to the courtyard, there they were, all three happily playing together. And yet, she'd heard it. She was right outside the room, and she'd heard the sound clearly.

Cindy didn't tell Mohammed about the weird sounds. She knew he would overreact, and tell her that she needed someone there with her. Cindy didn't want a live-in maid, and she didn't want any family members moving in with her. She wasn't in the mood to put up with any of them. Mohammed's sons were urging her to tell him, but Cindy told them no, she didn't want to bother him with it. She was enjoying having her own house, she didn't want to worry him, so she said nothing.

Then one winter night it became too much. Cindy was cooking an early dinner, wanting to get out of the kitchen before it got dark, and the eerie feeling came over her. She felt something watching her. Bringing their dinner into the little family room, she sat down with the kids to watch television. As they were eating, Cindy began to hear a hollow banging sound like someone was pounding from inside the walls – but the walls were made of cinderblocks. *Doong, doong, doong ....* Not wanting to alarm the kids, Cindy ignored the noise and turned up the volume on the television. But the noise kept up, slowly getting louder, until finally she called Jassim.

"You better get over here. Something's going on."

The entourage was at her gate moments later, and this time they insisted she call Mohammed and tell him what was happening.

"I know," he said. "I've been hearing noises, too." Strange things had been happening when he got up for dawn prayer, but he hadn't said anything to Cindy figuring, if she wasn't bothered by it, he didn't mind. "You need to get your things and get out of the house, NOW."

Cindy resisted. "No! I'm not leaving. This is my house." She didn't want anyone or anything driving her out of her own house. Suddenly the booming in the wall changed to a keening, shrieking, terrifying *DEEDEEDEEDEEDEEEEEEEE!* Everybody heard it. Zamzam and Ali, the kids, the stepsons – they were all there, and they all agreed later. They had all heard it. It was real. It seemed like, when she insisted on staying, she was being told, *Okay, so you're not leaving? WE'LL GET YOU OUT OF HERE!"*

"Okay, okay, I will leave! I WILL LEAVE!"

When Cindy and Mohammed told the owners that they were moving out, they let them out of the lease, refunded the balance of the rent with no questions asked, and immediately afterward put the house up for sale. Cindy couldn't explain what had happened; if it hadn't happened to her, she wouldn't have believed the story. Maybe she'd done something wrong to anger a *djinn,* or maybe the owners had decided to sell the house after it was rented, and put some magic on it to make Cindy move out. She would never be able to explain it, except to say that it happened.

"Come and live in my house," Auntie Fatima said when she heard the story. "Why do you want to rent, anyway? I am moving in with my daughter soon. Then you can have the whole house – rent free." Fatima's house was close enough to make Zamzam happy. Her husband had died, and she was going to live with her daughter in Bahrain. It was the perfect solution. Cindy was grateful. For the hundredth time, she thought about how much she wished that Fatima, instead of Zamzam, could have been her mother-in-law.

Cindy was thinking that she had seen enough black magic and *djinn*, but a few weeks after she moved to Fatima's a neighbor came over with a problem and a request. Her husband had taken a second wife, and he'd gone to Dubai to live with her.

It was written in the Quran that if a man had more than one wife – he could have up to four – he must provide for them equally in all ways. But this almost never happened. How could it? There would be jealousy and competition between the wives, as the first wife was naturally cast aside and the husband was lured away by the new wife's charms.

This neighbor wanted her husband back. Maybe she still loved him, or maybe it was hurt pride. "I want you to take me to someone who will make magic so that my husband will love me more than his new wife," she told Cindy. She wanted Cindy to drive her to see a fortune teller who would give her guidance on love and tell her how to get her husband to come back. "I'm telling you," she said knowingly when Cindy was skeptical, "it works. You will see."

Cindy went along with it, mostly out of curiosity. They drove to the house of an Afghani man. The neighbor handed him an envelope of money, which the fortune teller took and hid somewhere within his loose clothing. Then he recited some words, and gave the jilted wife a bag holding an amulet containing a secret mixture. It would ward off evil and cure problems between a husband and wife.

"Hang this on a tree," he said. "Every time the wind blows, his heart will beat for you." That night the woman hung the amulet, and the wind blew all night. The very next day, her husband came back to Khorfakkan asking her to let him return, and telling her that he loved her and missed her. The spell had worked, and in only one night.

Cindy was amazed, but the neighbor just shrugged and said, "What? You think it doesn't work? I tell you, it works!"

Chapter 13: Learning Arabic

Cindy was having a dream. A funeral procession was passing by the house. She kept asking who had died, but no one would say who it was. It was one of the neighbors who had been sick. But who? No one was crying. Usually, you would see the family of the deceased quietly weeping, and that way you knew who it was. Suddenly Cindy felt herself beginning to cry, and then Mohammed's cousin, who was beside her in the dream, began to cry as well. The procession moved on out of sight, toward the graveyard.

One Friday soon after the dream, when Zamzam and Ali had gone home after dinner, the telephone rang. It was Jassim, asking to speak to Mohammed. Hanging up the phone after a brief conversation, Mohammed said, "I have to go to my father's house. He is sick. We are going to the hospital."

How sick could he be, Cindy wondered? They'd just seen him and he was fine. Perhaps it was indigestion. The meat could be hard on an old person's stomach.

Later, Mohammed called from the hospital. "You must go to my mother's house," he said. "Tell her my father is going to die."

Muslims talked about death euphemistically. If someone had died, they would say "God gave you a long life." That meant "God has taken a life, but we take comfort in the lives that continue." A common response was "The rest is your life," meaning "May the unlived years be added to your life."

But Cindy didn't know how to express the idea that someone was going to die, but was not dead yet. She couldn't go to Zamzam and tell her that Ali Mubarak was dying, because she knew no way to express it in future tense. She could only tell her that Ali dies. That he was dead. What if she said it before it happened, and then somehow Ali lived? What would Zamzam think? What would she do?

Cindy went over to the house but didn't say the words that she knew were true, because they were not quite true yet. Others were there, waiting for news. The cousin was there, the one in the dream. As they waited, Cindy thought of Ali's life, and Zamzam's. They had been married for over forty years. Mohammed was born within a year, with two more boys to follow. It was a typical union, arranged for the pleasure and convenience of the husband, and to provide him with sons.

Zamzam was probably about fourteen when they wed, and Ali was some twenty years older. Nobody knew exactly how old they were, because there were no birth certificates to prove it. When they had been issued their Emirati passports, the officials had made up birth dates out of thin air. Fatima and Zamzam, sisters, had identical birthdates, although Fatima was clearly older than Zamzam. But nobody knew exactly how much older.

Most Emirati families were larger than Zamzam and Ali's. Why hadn't they had more children? Cindy could only guess. Perhaps she'd had miscarriages. Or perhaps she'd stopped conceiving. Zamzam complained about her husband bitterly and often. When Fatima's husband died, Zamzam had commented with some resentment, "Now that your husband is dead, you can do what you want."

But did Zamzam listen to and obey Ali? Not unless it suited her. More often, she found a way to do as she pleased. How much did Zamzam love Ali, if at all? Did she even know what love was? For so many of the older generation, marriage was about having sex and producing children. They were chosen by their husbands' mothers. Love had nothing to do with it; the bride and groom didn't know each other at all when they married. Although forced marriage was against the law, there was often pressure. If it grew into love, that was good, but that wasn't always what happened. Now, as a widow, Zamzam would never marry again. People would talk. "What? Didn't she get enough sex with her first husband?" No, once Ali was gone, Zamzam would be finished with marriage.

But Cindy's marriage was different. She and Mohammed had married for love, and as her love for Mohammed had grown, so had her love for his family. She didn't want to lose Ali. She didn't want Mohammed to lose his father, as she had already lost hers. Cindy began to cry and, as she did, the cousin beside her began to weep quietly as well. Just like in the dream. Then the telephone rang.

When a Muslim has died, the family gathers and reads the prayers for the dead from the Quran. Ali Mubarak had died of a heart attack. Sitting at the funeral with the Quran in her lap, Cindy was struggling to read the funeral prayers.

I've been here fourteen years, she thought. *I need to learn to read the Quran.*

Reading and writing Arabic was difficult. Cindy had learned the alphabet long ago, but knowing the letters was only the beginning. The problem with Arabic was that a letter was different depending on whether it was at the beginning, middle, or end of the word. And there were no books available in both English and Arabic. Most of Cindy's reading was in English, bringing books from home. And books in English had been getting easier to get in the UAE every year, so there was no need to learn Arabic to have something to read. Her Arabic skills consisted mostly of reading labels, signs, menus, and children's comic books. *Majid* was easy reading and helpful for everyday conversation, but it didn't help at all with the classical Arabic of the Quran.

The only time she'd ever needed to read formal Arabic was when someone died, and she'd been able to get by but it was a struggle. Now her children were getting older, and Aminah and Aisha were learning to read and write Arabic in school. Cindy was worried that, because they spoke English with her at home, her children would be at a disadvantage. She needed to be able to help them but how could she if she couldn't read and write Arabic herself? One of Mohammed's many cousins worked for the Social Development Center, which offered adult education classes. "Come to the Center and learn Arabic," she said.

The classes were taught separately, as Cindy expected. She'd gotten used to the way everything was separate for men and women – mosques, social gatherings, schools. There were even ladies' lines in stores and designated ladies' waiting areas in hospitals and government buildings. It was nice to be able to go to right up to the ladies' window in the post office and, if there were men in line, they would respectfully stand aside and let her go before them.

The Arabic classes were remedial – they weren't for educated foreigners like Cindy; no such classes existed in Khorfakkan. Maybe they were available in Dubai or Abu Dhabi, where there were new international colleges and universities, with expats working there and wanting to learn some Arabic. There simply wasn't the demand in Khorfakkan. The future men's and women's colleges for Emirati nationals hadn't been built in Fujairah yet. These classes were for uneducated, illiterate locals who hadn't even a basic education.

Cindy wore the *abaya* and *shayla*, but she didn't veil her face as many of the local women in the classroom did. Even though the room was filled with only women, some never removed their veils – just in case a man might walk in, or the shadow of a man might pass by a window. Cindy stood out from the rest – everyone could see her white skin. When she spoke in her now-fluent Arabic, the North Carolina accent she would never lose gave her speech a twang that other people tried to identify. She could feel their curiosity. But she wasn't a stranger to everyone; she knew many of the people there and many more knew who she was, even if they hadn't met. She was the American wife they'd heard of, if not met.

For the next two years, while the girls were in school, Cindy left Faisal with the part-time maid while she went to classes from eight in the morning until noon. For curious, intelligent Cindy, the classes were fun, if not always challenging. It was a complete academic program, with classes in math, science, and religion as well as English and Arabic. It was like going back to elementary school, but she was learning everything in Arabic. Everything was easy for Cindy because, unlike her classmates, she knew how to study. She'd already been educated; the others had no concept of studying.

The most challenging part was the English class, and only because it was so boring. Because it was remedial literacy, English was required to get a certificate to move on to the next level. Cindy wearied of hearing English words mispronounced by the teachers, perpetuating the mistakes that she'd heard every day for years. They were teaching it wrong, but if they asked for a volunteer to pronounce a word and Cindy raised her hand and volunteered, often as not she'd be told she was wrong – and it was her own native language. Arabic speakers had a pattern of making the same mistakes. They weren't used to the wide variety of vowel pronunciations in English. So "duck" was the same as "dock." Oh, well.

Then there was the cheating. Lying was forbidden in their religion, but cheating didn't seem to be in the same category. Cheating and copying was blatant and rampant, and although teachers tried to stop it, everybody did it. She knew that people were cheating off her because, on one test, she'd carelessly put down a wrong answer and the woman in the next seat copied it. The teacher knew immediately. "You have this answer because Cindy has this answer!" she scolded the woman. "You copied the wrong answer!" Cindy only smiled and shrugged.

The English tests were so easy they made Cindy want to cry. It was a matching game, with first grade words on one side and pictures on the other. Everyone knew that Cindy had all the answers, and they expected her to help them on the tests. She'd try to finish as quickly as possible, to keep people from copying, but she wasn't allowed to leave until half of the testing time was over, which was always an excruciating hour or even longer. Meanwhile, everybody in the room was surreptitiously trying to get her attention. There should be special circumstances for people like her, she thought. She shouldn't have to sit there, with everyone bugging her for answers. But it didn't occur to the teachers, because there was nobody like her. There never had been and there never would be again.

Finally, the peer pressure became too much and Cindy wrote one answer on an eraser, then watched as it was passed all around the classroom. *Well. At least I helped them with that one. Now maybe they'll leave me alone.*

After two years of classes, to her great satisfaction, Cindy graduated first in her class. She couldn't help but be proud, knowing that all the others were native speakers yet she had excelled. Now she could take the advanced classes if she wanted to continue with her Arabic language education. But she would have to go at night, and she wasn't willing to leave the children. She needed to be home with them, helping with their school lessons and making sure they were keeping up. Reluctantly, she gave up on the idea of taking advanced Arabic.

Cindy was right in her concern that her children would be challenged in school. While Mohammed was gone all week, she spoke to her children mostly in English. When he came home for the weekend, they spoke a mixture of English and Arabic. For years, the relatives, especially Zamzam, had criticized her for speaking to them in English.

"They are Emirati! Why you talk to them in so much English? You speak too much English. They need Arabic." But Cindy was steadfast in her conviction that they should learn English and learn it well. She wanted them to be fluent English speakers, and she didn't care what Zamzam or any of the others said. Instead, she made it a point to speak English to her kids when Zamzam would hear it. They were her kids, and nobody was going to tell her what language to speak with them. While the other kids struggled to learn English with no help at home, her kids would have no trouble. They would be different, yes. The other kids would notice it. They were American as well as Emirati. But in this world, living in the UAE where there were so many opportunities, that would be a good thing.

1995

Gladys with Aminah, Aisha, and Faisal, Mocksville, 1995

In the UAE, dressed for a celebration

Aisha and Faisal at Grandma Gladys's home in Mocksville

Chapter 14: Umm Faisal

1998

"You cannot be American. Your Arabic is too good." The teachers were surprised to see the white lady speaking Arabic.

"Yes, I am American," Cindy always said with a smile. "I've been living here for years. That's how I learned Arabic."

As a mother in Khorfakkan, Cindy's routine was no different than it would have been if she were raising a family in Mocksville. There, she would have been actively involved in the schools, volunteering in the classroom, signing up to help with events, and helping her kids with homework and classroom projects. She would have been a favorite with the teachers. In Khorfakkan, she was doing all those things, but she was virtually the only mother doing it. Plus, she was American, and she spoke fluent Arabic. She was unique.

When Aminah had started kindergarten, Cindy noticed that mothers were a rare sight. Many children were walked to school by their nannies, who left them off outside the front doors while the nannies gathered in groups to gossip. Others were brought by their fathers in large SUV's, roaring up in front of the school to drop them off any place they could pull over. The children would pile out, the father careening off almost before the door was closed. It was a wonder he didn't run them over. Less fortunate children used the local bus system. Cindy felt sorry for them, riding to school without air conditioning on the sweltering bus.

Cindy drove her kids to school each day, starting when Aminah was in kindergarten. Parking the car and walking them in, she enjoyed meeting and talking with the teachers, who were all Arab except for the expat music and P.E. teachers. She was shy in the beginning, but by the time Aminah was in third grade and Aisha was in first, she was speaking fluently, almost like a local, and the basic reading and writing skills she'd learned at the adult school had blossomed. Aminah and Aisha went to the girls' school, and now Faisal was in preschool at the boys' school.

Seeing the neighbor children riding the bus or being left outside by the nanny, Cindy offered to drive them herself when she took her own children. Soon word got around that Umm Faisal was reliable, on time, and would take care of the children, seeing them safely into the school, going to get them when school was over, and not leaving them at home unless there was a responsible adult to look after them. Eventually, she was driving two loads of children to and from school every day, one to Faisal's school and one to the girls'. She'd worked out an efficient route and schedule. People were paying her handsomely – more than she asked for. And they gave her gifts. Cindy was making 3,000 dirhams a month – about $900 – and was also rewarded with gifts of food, flowers, and trinkets.

Whenever she had an opportunity, she would linger, talking with the teachers and staff about what was happening in the school. Yasmeen, her friend and neighbor from the apartment, had been Aminah's first-grade teacher. She told Cindy stories about what happened with the kids in school during the day. Whenever there was an event coming up – a performance, lecture, or informational meeting, Cindy knew about it and went, no matter what it was. Often, she was one of just two or three mothers – unless there was food.

Umm Faisal was finally beginning to feel like she was part of the community in her own right. She was well known around the schools and around town, and she was respected for her ability to speak and read the local language. One day, lingering in the school office, she happened to pick up a copy of a notice that was going out to the parents and read it over.

"You know," she said, "there's a mistake in this."

"What!" the school social worker said. "Of course, all these Arab people here and it's you who finds the mistake."

Every school had a social worker, whose job it was to work as a liaison between the school and the parent community. When a child was having difficulty learning, or was misbehaving in school, the social worker would seek out the parents. It was also the social worker's job to plan school events and the meetings and invite parents to attend, working with the Mothers' Council, their version of a PTA.

"Excuse me, Umm Faisal?" the social worker asked one day. "Do you want to participate on our Mothers' Council?"

Cindy hesitated, shy about taking a leadership role. Would she be able to perform the duties? Would she be able to communicate well enough? Would she understand what was required? "Do you think I can do it?" she asked.

"Of course, you can! Absolutely."

In no time, Cindy found herself immersed in projects. There were posters to be made for informational meetings, events to organize. Environmental Day was a community cleanup day, there were food and clothing drives for the poor, and decorating for National Day and other holidays.

When Faisal started first grade, his school social worker asked Cindy to be on the Mother's Council there. "Oh," Cindy said, "but I'm already on the one at the other school."

"No problem! You can be on ours, too. Please, could you help us?" Thus, Cindy found herself on two Mothers' Councils.

When she wasn't busy with Council duties or helping the kids with their homework, Cindy was on the computer. Just as she was one of the first women drivers in Khorfakkan, Cindy was one of the first computer users. Using dial-up service, she got onto the Internet and stayed up until all hours of the night, teaching herself through trial and error. She spent hours surfing and, to her delight, could get American news in real time, satisfying her craving for up-to-the-minute information from back home in America. She could read the Davie County Enterprise Record online. No longer would she be finding things out after the fact. She could find out what was happening on her favorite soap operas.

One of her friends in North Carolina had told her about this new thing that everybody was getting called email. Now, expensive phone calls were a thing of the past. She could keep in touch with everyone by sending an email. It would go out while she was awake and they were asleep, and they could wake up and send her a reply. Every morning, Cindy couldn't wait to turn on the computer and check her email. As one of the first email users, she got her own name as her email address: "cindylou." Her two separate worlds had merged.

Not only did she have Internet, but she had cable television and she and the kids had Showtime and The Disney Channel. Aisha was in love with Power Puff Girls, and everything Disney. The cable company regularly ran contests, drawings, and promotions, and Cindy entered every one, becoming a frequent winner while the locals were just catching on.

One of her prizes, from The Disney Channel, was a brand-new Compaq computer that came with a program called Power Point. Cindy had spent a lot of time playing on the old computer before, but it was nothing compared to the hours she spent learning Power Point. She played with templates, fonts, styles, colors. She practiced creating slide shows with graphics she found in her searches. Soon she discovered the animation features. She was teaching herself, but when she had questions she did have someone one to ask. It wasn't Mohammed, who knew next to nothing about computers. It was her stepsons, who were in college. They were always encouraging.

"If you know English," they told her, "you know computers. No problem, you can learn it."

The schools were getting computers too, but most of the teachers and staff didn't know what to do with them. They came to rely on "Sindiya," as they now called her, with her American ingenuity, as their trouble shooter. A printer wouldn't print, call Sindiya to fix it. A program wouldn't work, Sindiya could figure it out. The Internet was out, call Sindiya. Usually it was just a matter of restarting, reinstalling, changing a cartridge, or even adding paper. No matter how simple the solution, Sindiya was a genius, saving the day.

"She is the expert! What would we do without Sindiya?" she heard several times a week, and it always made her smile and shake her head.

"It's simple." But it wasn't simple to them.

The posters Cindy was making for the parent education meetings became Power Point presentations, the first ones being on healthy teeth and good nutrition. Most Emirati people had a diet overloaded with starches and sweets, poor dental hygiene, and decaying teeth. Shelves in the new "hypermarkets" were filled with an infinite variety of imported cookies and biscuits, cakes, candies, chips and crisps, and sugary drinks. The selection was constantly expanding. One day Cindy spotted an old favorite, Mountain Dew. Oh, how she loved Mountain Dew. They had a similar drink called Oman Dew, but it wasn't the same. She bought some for everyone to try, and they loved it. Even Zamzam would ask for it, saying, "I want the drink that *she* drinks."

The Bedouin in the desert had eaten dense, sweet dates and drank naturally sweet, nutritious camel milk. In settled areas like Khorfakkan, local people traditionally ate rice and meat, fava beans, hummus and olives, and locally grown squash, cucumbers, greens, and tomatoes. Older people still preferred local food. The workers from Afghanistan, Pakistan and India flocked to buy inexpensive *shawarma,* flatbread wraps stuffed with spit-roasted meat, French fries, and a bit of vegetable, sold at little hole-in-the-wall places which opened in the early evening. But the young people flocked to the fast food places, crowding into them as soon as they opened. Hardee's, the only restaurant in Mocksville when Cindy had left, was the first American fast food restaurant in Khorfakkan, followed soon by Pizza Hut, McDonald's, Baskin Robbins, Subway, and KFC. The result of the new diet was already evident in rotten teeth, obesity, and a spike in diabetes.

Cindy made a Power Point about tooth decay and dental hygiene with photos of rotten teeth and gums, and healthy teeth and gums. She added graphics of toothbrushes, teeth, how to brush, how to floss. Only a handful of people came to the meeting, but they laughed as the toothbrush flew into view, and yellow teeth were replaced with gleaming white ones. She found a picture of a smiling child in a dentist's chair – which the people in the room had never seen, having never been to a dentist. One slide said, "BRUSH YOUR TEETH THREE TIMES A DAY." Another said, "FLOSS EVERY DAY." She had another slide with the names of local dentists and their telephone numbers. The images zoomed in, faded out, and melted into one another. Her tiny audience was entertained.

The school nurse, as she handed out toothbrushes, said, "You know, that was the best presentation I've ever seen. Can you come give it at another school? And can you make one on nutrition?" And so, Cindy's role and responsibilities grew.

The presentation that Cindy took most seriously, but the one she felt would probably not draw a big audience, was on the importance of learning English. She'd gotten so much criticism from Mohammed's family for speaking English at home to her own children, she wondered if the parents at the school held the same view. To her surprise, the house was packed – so much so that she was a bit intimidated. Word about Umm Faisal's Power Point presentations had gotten around.

Her uneasiness was short-lived. Soon people were laughing and talking as she went through slide after slide, explaining the usefulness of English in her fluent Arabic. There were slides showing countries where English was the official language; another showing that it was the language of business. Other slides showed the many books, films, and other entertainment that were in English, and how English was the language of technology and the Internet. Cindy pointed out that most Internet content – where she had found all her information, her pictures, everything – was in English. She showed them the results of a search she'd done in Arabic, and then the same search in English. There was no comparison.

"You see," she concluded, speaking in perfect local Arabic with the slight North Carolina twang that would never completely fade away, "how much more you can do if you know English. That is why it's important that your children learn English. And you should learn it, too." The room was buzzing as the crowd listened – and talked – a hallmark of an engaged Arab audience.

Cindy's Arabic had become so good that people sometimes didn't believe she wasn't a local, especially over the telephone. Calling to ask about cable television, she'd explained what she wanted, and the salesman on the other end of the line had asked for her name.

"Cindy Davis."

"If you want to give me a false name, lady," the salesman said, annoyed, "don't give me an English name."

"No, no," Cindy said in Arabic. "That really is my name. Cindy Davis. I'm American."

"No, no. Impossible. I do not believe it."

Cindy was annoyed. "How do you know it's impossible?"

"It is not possible because Americans cannot speak Arabic," the salesman said.

"Look, mister. I've been here for a long time."

"Doesn't matter. Even if you say you've been here for a hundred years," the man replied, "Americans cannot speak Arabic. They don't have the tongue for it."

This was too much. "Ok, whatever. You can believe what you want to believe."

"Prove to me that you are American," he challenged.

How dare he? But she couldn't resist the challenge, knowing how shocked he would be. Still speaking Arabic, she baited him, saying, "Why do I have to prove anything to you? If you want to believe me, then believe me. If you don't want to, you don't have to believe me."

Switching to English, the salesman said, "Ok, let me ask you this. Would you like to subscribe to the Orbitz channel?" He told her the price.

"No, thank you, not at this time. It's too expensive," she replied. In English.

"Wow. You are American. How can you speak such good Arabic? I am from Jordan and I can't speak the Arabic they speak here as well as you."

"Well," Cindy said with satisfaction, "you learned to speak Arabic your way, and this is the way I learned to speak, from them. That's why I sound like them. You learned it from your British teachers, and I learned it here, with an American accent. I guess that makes me sound like them." Suddenly she felt a camaraderie with the man on the other end of the line. Arabic was not one language, the same everywhere, any more than English sounded the same everywhere.

At Faisal's school, Cindy found a friend in Jameela, the mother of four boys whose son Ahmed was Faisal's age. Jameela was beautiful, funny, fun, and full of ideas. She lived close to Fatima's house, and little Ahmed joined Cindy's carpool, with Jameela often along for the ride to visit and plan things with Cindy. There was always something going on. The children were assigned projects for every theme week, every festival, every holiday. There was Traffic Week, Water Week, Red Crescent

Week, Date Festival, Arabic Poetry Week, International Week, National Day.

Cindy and Jameela were a dream team, brainstorming together on their children's projects. Jameela was the idea person, and Cindy knew how to make it happen. A Google search produced directions on how to make anything. She'd always been crafty, and on trips home she brought back craft supplies she couldn't find in Khorfakkan. Suitcases came back filled with pipe cleaners, popsicle sticks, tissue paper, craft paper, glue guns, glitter, sequins, beads, buttons, ribbons, paints, fabrics, felt, wax, and on and on. She and Jameela would plan the project and work on it together – with the kids helping, of course.

Their favorite thing was building dioramas and models. For Red Crescent Week, which was like American Red Cross Week, they built a model refugee camp. Starting with a piece of plywood, they fashioned miniature tents, playgrounds for children, outdoor kitchens, dining areas, and corrals for animals. Traffic Week's project was a model of a crosswalk, showing how to safely cross a busy street. First, second, and third place awards were given for every project, and Faisal and Ahmed were consistent first-place winners. Their projects were always the best. It was the attention to detail.

Faisal excelled at projects, but his marks in English were another story. He had decided early on that he didn't want to be seen by his Emirati friends as an American. That would set him apart; it would make him different from the other boys. He refused to speak English at school, which became a problem in his English classes. It got to the point where one of his teachers thought he didn't know any English.

"What, do you want to fail English?" Cindy asked, exasperated. "You have to speak English in English class, or your teacher will fail you." Although she was frustrated, she had to laugh about it with Mohammed. How ironic was that? Her son could fail English.

The UAE government had cultivated a strong sense of nationalism and pride in being Emirati. Anyone with a foreign mother was different, and some people looked down on "half-Emiratis." Mohammed was known among his friends as "Mohammed the American," and their children were "the American" as well. Faisal did everything he could to be like his Emirati cousins and friends, and Aminah quietly fit in among her peers. Then there was Aisha.

Outspoken, boisterous Aisha was having trouble fitting in. She had dark hair, but with her fair skin, strawberry lips like Cindy's, and her Uncle Randy's features, she looked American to the other kids. She'd grown up spending half her summers playing with her boy cousins in North Carolina, free and fearless. When she came home, she wanted to play with the boys.

"No," Mohammed told her. "You can't play with boys."

"Why not?" Aisha pouted.

"We don't do that here," her father said, and it ended there.

Aisha's spirit, outspoken ways, and desire to fit in got her into trouble beginning in first grade. Some old fish bones from when Khorfakkan had been a fishing village were dug up at the construction site next to the school. Rumors began to fly among the children that there was a graveyard next to the school, and it was haunted. Aisha, seeing a way to ingratiate herself with her peers – to be brave, admired – volunteered to go and get the bones. If she could prove that they were just fish bones, that there was no graveyard there, they would stop being afraid of the ghosts. She would be a superhero, and they would like her. They would be her friends. Calmly walking over to the pit, she gathered the bones and brought them back to the schoolyard.

"Look," she said as the other girls gathered around. "These are just fish bones. I proved it!"

"No!" one of the girls said. "There is a ghost behind you!" "The ghost is in you!" "You are the ghost now!" "There is a *djinni* in you!" Suddenly it had all gone wrong. Instead of making them her friends, she had driven them away. They were running away from her! "Don't come near us! You are a *djinni!*"

After that there was no way to fit in. Aisha became a loner. She sat alone at lunch. She worked alone on projects. When it came to P.E., she didn't want to be on a team if they didn't want her. "Just give me my exercises, and I'll do them by myself," she told the teacher.

Cindy was at the school often, and she knew what was happening but there was nothing she could do. She couldn't intervene; her daughter's social problems were her own. Aisha had brought so much of it upon herself. She had Mohammed's outgoing personality, Cindy's stubborn streak, and perhaps a bit of Zamzam's petulance. Her temperament and her need to be recognized, combined with her love of all things American and her disdain for what she saw as the backwardness of her friends' Arab ways – it was a social disaster. The girls at school were just like American kids, like kids everywhere. If you were different, you were an outsider. If they were jealous of you, you were an outcast.

Cindy's heart hurt for her daughter, but she trusted that it would all work out for the best. She told Aisha to be patient and to wait it out. Trust in God that things would change. "Look," she said, "you just have to be yourself and do what you know is right. If people like you, fine, but if they don't then that's their choice. You can't change them, and they can't change you. You just wait, and everything will turn out the way it's supposed to." Aisha was trying too hard; she pushed herself on others. Cindy truly believed her words. Trust in God's will. Things would work out the way they were supposed to.

Chapter 15: Nine-Eleven

2001

It was a typically hot, humid September day. Everyone was weary of the heat, looking forward to October and the cooler season. Cindy was picking up some relatives in her SUV, the air conditioning blasting. They were going to call on a distant cousin whose son had died in a car crash. They were almost there when Cindy's mobile phone jangled. Mohammed. She answered.

"There has been an airplane crash into a building in New York," he said. "I don't know what is going on, but I wanted to let you know. You should turn on the TV."

"Oh, no." Cindy was anxious to get the details but they were almost there, rounding the last corner. "I'm going to the funeral. I'll find out what's happening when I get home, *inshallah*." They hung up. "We have to make this quick," she told the other ladies, "something's happening in the United States. There's been a plane crash."

"Where is happening?" one of the ladies asked. Her son was at the Cleveland Clinic getting treatment for diabetes.

"Don't worry," Cindy told her. "It's in New York. It's far away."

Cindy fidgeted through the prayers, her mind back in America. Even if it was something small, she wanted to know. The thought of something happening, and her not knowing about it, her missing something, anything, drove her half crazy. Why couldn't they hurry a little more? After what seemed like an eternity, she herded the others back into the car, telling them she needed to get home and turn on the news. She drove as fast as she dared. She couldn't get home soon enough, all the while thinking: *What am I missing? What am I missing?*

Home at last, Cindy turned on the television and even before the picture came up, the words she heard the CNN reporter say made her heart freeze: *terrorist attack.* Then the smoldering twin towers of the World

Trade Center in New York City came into view on the screen. What was this? What was happening? The news anchors were describing the scene in barely composed voices, using words like "chaos," "horrific," "terrible," and "nightmare." There was a jagged, gaping hole near the top of one building, several floors were blackened, and thick black smoke was billowing out. The other building looked like the entire top was on fire. The news anchors were speaking with reporters at the scene on the ground. Everyone was still trying to figure out what was happening.

Cindy sat down, trying to absorb what she was seeing. It looked like a disaster movie. Was this real? What was going on? *This is what Mohammed was calling about. A plane crashed into one of the twin towers in New York.*

The regular morning news shows had been in progress when they were interrupted with the first reports of a plane crash into one of the World Trade Center towers. Then, as the reporters, the morning show anchors, and all of America had watched, another plane had slammed into the other tower. The television cameras had captured it live, and now Cindy watched it repeated, again, again, and again. She would watch it dozens of times over the next days and weeks, but there was much more to come as she watched now, live. Fires raged on the upper floors. Firemen were on the scene, but it was unclear how many people were trapped, and how many may have been killed when the planes hit.

So much was happening. People in the streets were standing and watching the burning towers. Some were walking, dazed, some injured, some sobbing. They were saying that people were jumping to their deaths from the highest floors. Cindy heard that the Pentagon had been hit by a plane, as well. All flights over the U.S. were grounded, and the ones in the air ordered to land immediately.

Then, as Cindy watched in disbelief, the top of the South Tower began to crumble. *Oh, my God. Oh, my God. Oh, my God. No. No.* Slowly, and then gaining speed, the tower collapsed upon itself, leaving a column of falling dust that became a mushroom cloud, spreading out and up. The building had collapsed like a house of cards.

The scene looked like it was filmed in black and white, like an old movie about something that was happening on another planet. Everything was fuzzy, grey. It was chaotic. Unreal. But it was real.

Cindy sat, mesmerized, as a feeling of gloom swept over her. Inevitably, tragically, the North Tower collapsed beside its fallen twin. How many people were dead? No one could guess. What about people on the ground? How many were hurt? Where were they? Where could they go? How could they escape the choking dust that was everywhere in downtown Manhattan?

Then came the report of another plane crash, this one onto an open field in Pennsylvania. *What is going on? What will happen next? When will this end?* Cindy just sat. She couldn't move, worried about her mother, her brothers, her sister. Her nephews and nieces. In America.

Mohammed called. Earlier, he hadn't known that it was the World Trade Center that had been hit. But he knew now, and like everyone around the world, he was watching as events unfolded. If this was a terrorist attack, as they were already saying, they both knew that everything would be different. There had been a growing distrust of Muslims before. There had been attacks. Ships, embassies, airplanes. But never, ever, like this. Never in America. On American soil. Cindy knew in her heart, just as every other American knew, that in that instant when the first plane hit, the world had changed. Things would be different in America.

Aisha was eleven. As she watched her mother talking to her father on the phone, she knew that something bad was happening. Her mommy was so serious, so quiet, talking under her breath so that Aisha couldn't hear.

"What is it, Mommy? What's happening?"

"Never mind. You'll find out about it later. Go and play."

"Can we go to Baskin-Robbins?"

"No, not right now."

"Later?"

"I don't know."

Why does mommy look like she's going to cry?

Cindy sat up all night, glued to the television, watching the aftermath unfold. The news replayed the same scenes over and over as bits and pieces of information filtered in. It was like an obsession; she couldn't turn it off. She couldn't stop watching the planes hitting the towers, the plumes of smoke rising into the crystal-clear New York sky, listening to the comments of incredulous observers all over New York as they recorded the developing disaster on their cell phones. "Oh, my God." Or, ironically, "Wow." As if it were a spectacle, like a firework show. The reality of it, the lives lost and changed forever, was impossible to grasp in those first few moments. Cindy relived it over and over, and always some small, childish part of her wished that this time the outcome was different. She wished that the next piece of news would be something good. But it never was.

The next morning, her heart heavy, Cindy drove the kids to school. The teachers were as shocked as she was, and sympathetic. "We are sorry," was all they could say. They didn't say much to the children about what had happened – let the parents do that at home. As an American, Cindy was reeling from the shock of the attacks. She grieved for the people in the towers, and their families. She grieved for New York, for the lost firemen, for the destruction. The people in the airplanes, and on the ground at the Pentagon. The loss of innocence. America had been attacked, on American soil. And it was becoming more and more clear that it had been Muslim terrorists who had launched the attack. She told her children as much as they needed to know, but no more.

"America has been attacked. People crashed airplanes into buildings in New York and Washington D.C. Everyone in North Carolina is ok. We don't know yet who did it." Things would stay the same for them. It had happened in America, not Khorfakkan. The children were too young to understand. It was best to downplay it.

Everyone Cindy knew said it was a terrible thing. But after the attack, out on the Corniche, a group of people gathered and celebrated. Cindy was appalled. It was unbelievable, that people could be happy about such horrendous acts. The Khorfakkan police quickly rounded up and jailed the participants, and the newspaper printed a story condemning their actions, saying no one should ever celebrate such a thing. Still, it had deepened the wound.

Within a few days, the identities of the hijackers were released by the FBI. Of the nineteen men, fifteen were from Saudi Arabia, one was from

Egypt, one from Lebanon and two were from the UAE. Of those two, one was from Ras Al Khaimah and one was from Khorfakkan.

They had felt comfortably distant from it all, but once the hijacker from Khorfakkan was identified investigators came, asking questions. People were detained, interrogated, and sometimes jailed for weeks or even months. In such a small town, with so many interconnected families, everyone was suspected of knowing the hijacker. He was the son of a school principal, and had left sometime in 2000, telling his parents that he hoped to work with a charity group. His parents had heard from him once, then he had disappeared. It was hard to find anyone in town who didn't know the family. It was equally unlikely to find anyone who knew anything about the young man's activities. Somehow, he had been radicalized. Everyone had heard that this kind of thing was happening, it was growing. To mainstream Muslim people like Mohammed and his family, radical Islam was a problem, just as big a threat to them, to their peaceful lives, as it was to the non-Muslim world. Perhaps greater.

For Aminah and Faisal, 911 didn't influence their relationships with their peers. For Aisha, it was an end and a beginning. Just a day before the attacks, she had been showing off the shoes, jewelry, and a handbag that she'd brought back from the family's summer trip to Jordan and Syria. For once, the other girls at school had paid attention, gathering around, admiring her new things and asking questions. But the day after the attacks, walking into the classroom, Aisha felt something different. She said good morning and tried to talk to people, but no one would look at her. She sat in her seat, third row on the left, and one by one as the other girls entered they moved their chairs away. No one spoke to her, no one looked at her, and no one wanted to sit near her. At P.E., no one picked her for volleyball. At the end of the selection, she stood alone. And she made a decision.

I'm done. That's it. I'm finished trying to fit in. Nothing pleases them. I am tired of being ignored, made fun of, and bullied. No more begging to be one of them. From now on, I'm not doing anything for them. No more helping with homework, tests, nothing.

It was the end of the old, needy Aisha and the beginning of strong Aisha. She decided to take a page from her mother's book. If someone wanted to be her friend, fine. If not, fine. But if anyone tried to bully her, watch out. For the rest of the school year, Aisha forged and perfected her new persona. She was in her last year of primary school. Next year, she would be going to the middle school, and she could start over there. She would always remember 911 as America's tragedy that made her stronger. The shunning taught her that she didn't have to take it. She realized that she just needed to be herself. Aisha the American not only survived, she found a new power.

If it seemed at first that 911 wouldn't change things in their world, Cindy and Mohammed were wrong. In the United States, Muslims were being detained and interrogated. Mohammed's cousin, who was there with his son for the diabetes treatment, was held for questioning at the Chicago airport while leaving to come home to the UAE because his name and that of the hijacker from Khorfakkan were similar. Did he know him? He must know him. They were from the same town. Mohammed's cousin knew who the man was, he'd heard of him, but he didn't know anything about his activities. He was one of hundreds of relatives whom he'd barely met.

Hearing stories like this, Cindy began to realize that the summer trips to North Carolina were over. No longer would she be able to take the kids home. It was too risky. Every time Cindy entered the United States with her children and presented her American and their UAE passports, she was questioned. She was their American mother? Children born overseas to an American parent are U.S. citizens. Where were their American passports?

"They don't have American passports because it's not allowed in the United Arab Emirates," she always explained. "The UAE doesn't allow its citizens to hold more than one passport." It wouldn't matter after they were eighteen, but as they were minor children traveling with an American parent, they were supposed to have American passports. The American customs officers always let them through, but not without making Cindy feel like she was breaking a law.

She'd had the best of both worlds. Now, that life was gone. She and the kids wouldn't be able to spend cool, carefree summers in North Carolina. Gladys would have no more visits from her grandchildren. She would not see them growing up, playing alongside their cousins, running on the great green lawns and climbing in the trees.

While negative attitudes toward Muslims and Arabs were on the rise in United States, Cindy felt nothing but sympathy and acceptance from the people in Khorfakkan. She was proud to be American, but she wondered if she was accepted because they knew her so well – she'd been there for twenty years. Was it different for other American expats, the professionals who were working there? She asked around, but every American she spoke to said the same thing. "No, I don't feel threatened here. I feel perfectly safe. Safer, in some ways, than I do at home in the United States." In the UAE, street crime was rare.

Back in the United States, people didn't understand. They assumed that Americans in the Middle East were living among terrorists. They couldn't see that the Muslim life that Cindy was living in the UAE was based on peace and acceptance of all regardless of religion or culture. No one had pressured her to convert. Her husband and family, the entire community, was reeling in shock over what had happened. They condemned the actions of the terrorists. But they had no way to speak out about it to the rest of the world.

After 911, Cindy went home every three years. Each time, she heard the same questions. "What are people like there?"

"Well," Cindy would say, "you know that TV show, *The Beverly Hillbillies?* They're kind of like that." They looked so simple from the outside, but when you went inside their houses, everything was flashy. The money had come in, and people had a chance to make up for the simple life they'd had until then. They furnished their houses in style. If it was gold or it glittered, it was good. If it was carved and upholstered in velvet, they bought it. Gilt coffee and tea services. Crystal pitchers. Everything was glossy and new.

"What are the women like there?"

"They're pretty much the same as us," Cindy would say. "People are people. Emirati women, from the outside, are quiet and reserved. But get them in a room together, let the *abayas* come off, and watch out, they can get crazy!" Older ladies wore house dresses or caftans underneath their *abayas,* but the younger women and girls sported the latest designer fashions.

A Christian friend asked, "How can you live your life, knowing that there's nobody to save you? You don't have a savior."

"Why do you need someone to save you?" Cindy asked. "Why don't you trust that God is forgiving, and that your deeds and actions will take you to heaven?"

"But what if I don't do enough?"

"That's why you always have to be striving to do good things, to remember God. Don't do anything that makes you afraid, because in the end it's the balance of good and bad that will take you to heaven. Why do you need a savior? Why can't you just live your life, knowing that God will save you?"

Chapter 16: Dream House

2002

Auntie Fatima lived with her daughter, and Cindy lived in Fatima's house. It was not an unusual arrangement, and perfect as far as it went. There was one drawback – a huge one. It wasn't her house. She couldn't do anything to it. If she wanted to redecorate or remodel, she couldn't. No painting, no landscaping. Fatima didn't want to change anything. There was a messy Acacia tree right at the front door that was driving Cindy crazy. She wanted to take it out, or at least trim it back, but no. Fatima didn't want to.

Their finances had improved again. Cindy had wanted her own place for a long time. Zamzam had her house, Hassan and his large family had theirs, Abdulrahman's widow Maryam still lived in her house, and Mohammed's ex-wife Aisha, her second husband Mohammed Ali, and their eight children had a house – the one Aisha had kept in the divorce. How was it that, after twenty years of marriage, Cindy did not have her house? Sometimes it seemed, despite what she told herself about being grateful for what she had, that Mohammed had provided for everyone but her.

"Get him to buy you a house," friends and relatives urged. "Nag him until you get it. Now that he has money he can get another wife. Make him get you a house!"

But that wasn't Cindy's way. It would happen when it was meant to happen, if it was God's plan. Her reward had always been the appreciation Mohammed showed her. Once, when the kids were little and money was tight, they had needed shoes for school, and Cindy didn't have the money to pay for them. When Mohammed came home for the weekend, she planned to confront him, tell him that he had to do something. She needed more money. When he got home on Thursday evening, she waited to broach the subject. She didn't want to hit him with it right away. As they got into the car, just as she was formulating the words she would use to bring it up, Mohammed spoke.

"Honey," he said. "I was telling people about everything that is happening now, and I told them there is one thing that keeps me from going crazy. They asked what, and I said, 'It is my wife. She never complains. She is the best wife. She keeps me from going crazy.'"

Then Mohammed had looked over at her, and Cindy had to look away. *Oh, my God! I was just going to complain. I'm so glad I didn't say anything.* Remembering that day, Cindy decided that nagging and complaining wasn't the way to approach Mohammed about the house. Instead, she asked a simple question.

"We've been married twenty years, now. Is it time to think about moving out of Fatima's place and get a place of our own?"

Mohammed nodded, agreeing. "We have the money now. We will buy a house, *inshallah.*"

Emiratis avoided working with realtors, preferring to make deals directly. Why bother to involve another person and pay commission when you could post a notice that a house was for sale? Only expats hired realtors. But without a formalized system for listing homes, one never knew when an owner might be willing to sell. If you saw a house you liked, you asked the owner if he would sell, and you made an offer.

There was a house nearby, owned by the family of Zamzam's good friend. She was a very nice lady – Cindy wondered how such nice people could put up with cranky Zamzam. The house was rented out. Over the past few years there had been several people making offers, but the owners refused to sell, even when they got an offer of more than the house was worth. Mohammed was worried that if he made an offer it would be refused, like all the others. He didn't want to pay more than the house was worth. How much should he offer? What to do? He stressed, he worried, he fretted.

"Why are you worrying about this?" Cindy asked. "Look, if this is meant to be, it will happen. It's not in your hands; it's in God's hands. Why do you stress like this?"

Finally, Mohammed met with the owner, and offered him an amount he thought was fair. To their surprise, it was accepted without further negotiation. Perhaps they liked Mohammed because he was Zamzam's son? Or maybe they happened to need the money right then? Who knew? Only God. Somehow, at that moment when Mohammed decided to make the offer, the owners were ready to sell. It was meant to be.

It was meant to be, but not so fast. The renters were waiting for their own house to be finished, and although they knew the house had been sold, they didn't bother to move out. Or pay rent. There was no formal, written agreement between them and Mohammed so they simply stayed on, taking advantage of the situation. Cindy and Mohammed knew the people. After all, Khorfakkan was a small town; everyone knew everyone else. They wanted to be nice, but after several weeks Cindy was losing patience.

"You need to get them to move out," she told Mohammed.

"No, it's all right, I don't want to ask them to move," Mohammed said.

"Why not? It's our house. We bought and paid for it."

"Honey, please. Just be patient. I don't want trouble." Mohammed always wanted to keep the peace.

"Oh, all right," she sighed. "Fine."

But after several more weeks, Cindy was finally good and fed up. She decided to confront the tenants herself. "We want our house now," she told them, simply but firmly. "You are going to have to move out. We bought our house to live in, not rent. And by the way," she pointed out, "you aren't even paying us rent." In a week, they were gone.

Cindy had some changes in mind, and she hired the most trustworthy contractor she could find to do the renovations before they moved in. She'd done her research. There were too many contractors, plumbers, masons, and electricians in name, without the knowledge and experience, who didn't know what they were doing. She chose the contractor with the best reputation, who also happened to be the one who had built the house in the first place. Who would know better what to do, and how to do it? It seemed perfect, and she was excited to get started.

Cindy had lived in the UAE long enough to know what she wanted, and what she didn't want. She would enclose the courtyard in the middle of the house and make it the kitchen. Walls needed to be torn down or moved, rooms needed to be refinished. The roof would need replacing. Electrical outlets installed. And the bathrooms – there would be no "two-step" pit toilets in her house. She wanted a western-style toilet with a toilet tissue holder next to the spray hose in each of the bathrooms. She made up her list of specifications, and drew up an agreement with the contractor for the remodel. The price was 125,000 dirhams – about $32,000 U.S. The contractor began work, stripping the house down to a shell – and then left it that way for weeks, while he went to work on other jobs. There was a building boom, and the weeks turned into months. Finally, when he was ready to resume construction, the price of cement had skyrocketed.

"You need to pay more," he told Cindy. "It costs me more."

No way. Cindy thought. "Not my fault," she replied. "You took so long, and now the prices are higher. It's your fault for delaying the work. I will only pay you what we already agreed on. No more."

"I'm losing money!" he protested.

"That doesn't matter," she said. "You should have thought of that when you took off to go and work on another job. It's not my fault that prices are higher. Why should I pay more? If you had completed the job on time, you wouldn't be losing money."

"Your wife is crazy," the contractor complained to Mohammed. Compared to the local ladies, Cindy was crazy. No wife dealt with contractors, plumbers, electricians, and painters. Cindy did, and not only was she assertive, she knew what she was talking about. She had to tell the workers how to do their own jobs, to get things done the way she wanted them. It took a threat to call the police before the contractor grudgingly went back to work.

Cindy Lou Davis, who was raised alongside four brothers, knew how to deal with men. It didn't faze her. Mohammed was gone all week, and if she didn't handle things, they wouldn't get done. Mohammed knew better than to try to control her. Even when he was home, he wasn't exactly the handyman – more often, she was. He wasn't as bad as Hassan, who still had not learned how to change a light bulb. But whenever anything broke, Mohammed's first reaction was to call someone. He and Aisha were roughhousing one weekend, and they crashed against a bedframe and broke it. "I'll have to call someone to fix it," Mohammed said.

"No, wait," Cindy said, looking at the broken joint. "I can fix this."

"No way! You cannot fix it yourself."

"Yes, I can. Just go get me a couple of L-shaped brackets and some screws."

"My goodness, Honey," he said, watching his wife go about repairing the bedframe. His amazing American wife. She knew how to handle anything. She took care of everything. He never had to worry. *Mashallah,* what would his life be without her?

Cindy's dream house, from the street (above) and the courtyard

Chapter 17: Pilgrimage to Mecca

2003

Every Muslim is required, at least once in his or her lifetime, to make the holy pilgrimage, or *haj,* to Mecca during the last month of the shifting Islamic calendar. This year's *haj* coincided with the children's midterm break, and Cindy and Mohammed agreed that the timing was perfect. The February weather would be cool, the danger of heat stroke would be less, and Cindy would be without the worry of how the kids would get to and from school and who would oversee their homework. The kids would stay with "Bambam." Cindy could focus on her spiritual journey.

Most Emirati people made the *haj* in tour groups, booked through companies who made transportation arrangements, booked hotel accommodations, and provided guides to assist with the performance of the many complicated rituals. Cindy and Mohammed's Khorfakkan group included several ladies that Cindy already knew, easing her mind.

Still, she was nervous. She'd seen the *haj* procession on television many times with a million people, maybe even two million. They poured into Mecca from all corners of the earth, moving in a circle around the most sacred Muslim site in the world, the *Kaaba,* a huge cube covered in black silk. That was just one of many rituals, all very specific in their order and how they were to be done.

Cindy's real fear was the crowds. She'd always avoided crowds because they made her feel claustrophobic. Add to that the fact that everyone would be headed in the same direction, to perform the same actions. Some of the rituals required people to walk quickly or even run, and people were so crowded together that there had been widely reported trampling deaths in years past. How would she manage her fears? What if something happened? She had no choice but to place herself in God's hands. *Dear God,* she prayed as she boarded the plane, *please help me get through this.*

They flew from Dubai, and upon landing in Jedda they performed the ritual ablutions to purify their bodies. They changed into *ihram*, the garments they would wear when they performed the rituals of the *haj*. All pilgrims dressed the same, without regard to social standing or wealth. Kings walked alongside servants, all equal before God. The men wore two white lengths of cloth, one wound around the waist and the other draped over one shoulder, leaving the other shoulder bare. Cindy was dressed identical to most other women, who were required only to dress modestly. Most wore white *abayas* or dresses, making sure that their underclothes were white, so as not to show through, the fabric of the *abaya* thick enough not to reveal the shape of the body should the sun shine at a certain angle. Cindy's head was covered with a white *hijab*, and her sandaled feet were encased in socks. Her face, and those of all women, would remain bare, as required.

The next act of entering the state of *Iram* – holiness – was to declare their intentions to perform the pilgrimage by saying the words: *O Allah! I intend to perform Umrah. Please make it easy for me and accept it from me. Amen.* Cindy said the Arabic words in her heart, and she whispered them again and again. Her spiritual journey had begun.

Their group boarded buses – men in one, women in another – and headed east toward the city of Mecca, the birthplace of the Prophet Muhammad, open only to Muslims. They passed under the Quran Gate, an arch marking the official entrance to the city as the group prayed: "Here we come, O Allah, here we come!" Outside the window of the bus, the streets of Mecca were a sea of people, all dressed in white, all walking, walking, walking.

Dear God, Cindy thought. *What have I gotten myself into?*

Mecca was in a wide floodplain, hemmed in by mountains. It reminded Cindy of Khorfakkan without the seashore; the Red Sea was one hundred kilometers to the west. Rain was infrequent, totaling only five inches per year, but if it came in a deluge, the city flooded.

They dropped their belongings at the hotel, men and women bunking separately. Fortunately, Cindy was sharing with another lady from Khorfakkan who she already knew, saving her the stress of sleeping in a room with a total stranger. They then joined the mass of worshippers moving toward the *Masjid-al-Haram,* the Great Mosque of Mecca and largest mosque in the world, to perform the *tawaf* – the walk around the *Kaaba* that Cindy had seen so many times on television.

As they joined the throngs of worshippers, Cindy began to relax despite the crowds – maybe even because of them. As she became one of them and one with them, with Mohammed nearby, the streets felt less crowded. There was no pushing, no shoving, no jostling. They entered the massive, 88-acre mosque complex with the *Kaaba* at its center. The *Kaaba* was believed by Muslims to be the oldest mosque in the world, constructed in 2130 BC by Abraham and his son Ishmael who later became grandfather to the Prophet Muhammad. Thus, the *haj* dated to pre-Islamic times – back to the time of Abraham.

The number of pilgrims was rapidly increasing, and there was great need for better accommodations, security and crowd control. When Cindy and Mohammed made the *haj*, the mosque was undergoing its third major renovation and expansion since the 1950's. There were new developments and improvements underway in Arafat and Mina, as well as Mecca. Everywhere they went, they would encounter crowds and traffic normally associated with *haj* compounded by construction delays and detours.

Always striving to be prepared for anything, Cindy had brought three sets of *imrah* clothing. She knew she would be wearing them for many long hours each day. She had also brought a large handbag in which she carried fruit, just in case the food didn't agree with her. She was never one to complain, as others were already doing – the hotel accommodations were inferior, the food wasn't good. Cindy wasn't there for a holiday. She was there to become closer to God. If she had a place to sleep and some nourishment, she would be fine. And it was best to be prepared. The bus would have bottled water for them, but not snacks. She also made sure that she carried a spare battery for her cell phone, fully charged. Just in case.

The first ritual was the *tawaf.* After kissing the black cornerstone of the *Kaaba,* believers circled the silk-swathed cube seven times in a counterclockwise procession, signifying unity in the worship of one God. Because of the crowds, it was impossible to get to the stone, so instead Cindy and Mohammed's group had been told by their guide to raise a hand in its direction. During the procession, she and Mohammed became separated. Men performed their first three rotations quickly – as quickly as possible given the crowds – and the final four circuits more slowly, while the women maintained a slower pace throughout. Cindy didn't even notice, wrapped up as she was in her journey and her whispered prayers.

There were seven prayers, one for each circuit around the *Kaaba.* The last prayer spoke to Cindy's faith, and the last line to her heart.

O Allah! Make me content with what you have provided me with, and bless me with what you have given me.

She believed in a God who knew her faults and could forgive them. God alone would judge her. He had given her contentment. He had provided her a life with Mohammed and his family. He had given her children. He had blessed her with Auntie Fatima, who had shared her home with Cindy for five years. He had blessed her, finally, with her own house. It was up to Cindy to find contentment with those blessings from God, and not to ask why she didn't have more.

The next ritual was the *Sa'ey,* meaning to search. It was a reenactment of an event which occurred before the existence of the *Kaaba,* when Abraham was commanded by God to leave his wife Hajar and infant son Ishmael alone in the vast and uninhabited desert, trusting in God to provide for them. Hajar was nursing the infant, and Abraham left them with only a skin filled with water and a few dates. After the provisions were gone, Hajar's milk went dry and she and her baby both began to starve. She was forced to search for help, leaving her baby behind on the ground in the sand. There were two hills nearby. Hajar ran to the top of the first hill, Al-Safa, searching for some form of help in the desert beyond, but there was nothing. Then she went across to the other hill, Al-Marwah, but again there was nothing but desolation. Hajar ran back and forth seven times, climbing the two hills without respite before finally returning to Ishmael to find an angel breaking the ground with his heel, where a pure freshwater spring was bubbling to the surface. Digging a basin around the spring so that she could draw the water up with her hands, she created a well from that spring which still existed. It was called the Zamzam well. Before beginning the *Sa'ey,* Cindy drank holy Zamzam water that was provided in large chilled dispensers.

In the past, people had been trampled as the crowds tried to run between the two hills. Cindy traveled the path, now a paved corridor completely enclosed within the walls of the massive mosque. Women walked, and men were only permitted to run a short distance between two points designated by green posts. There were seven long prayers, praising God, declaring their belief in only one God, and asking for blessings.

Lastly, they found themselves in the basement of the mosque, the location of the Zamzam well. There were coolers all around the Great Mosque, so that people could drink the best water in the world, at any time. And always, there was a special prayer to be said when drinking this water from Heaven, which was said to satisfy both thirst and hunger and to be a cure for sickness.

The next morning after prayer, they boarded the bus for Mina. Just a few kilometers from the center of Mecca, it was nevertheless a long bus ride. They spent the day and night there, praying and sleeping in tents in preparation for the next day, which they would spend at Arafat.

On the third day, they boarded their buses, left Mina and made the 30-kilometer drive east to the desolate plain of Arafat for the *wuquf,* meaning "standing before God." It was a day of prayer and atonement for past sins, and listening to a sermon delivered from the Mount of Mercy, where Muhammad delivered his last sermon. This rite was one of the most important parts of the pilgrimage. Without it, their *haj* would be invalid.

After sunset, they left Arafat to return to Mina, but first stopped to spend the night at a place called Muzdalifah. Once again, they prayed far into the night, and gathered pebbles for the next day's ritual stoning of *Shaytan,* the devil, in Mina. Normally, when they did finally take some rest, they would have slept under the open sky but dark clouds had formed and it was beginning to rain. It was decided that they should go back to the hotel.

The *rami al-jamarāt,* or "stoning of the devil," is a reenactment of Abraham's pilgrimage to Mecca, when he was tempted by the devil three times, and all three times was instructed by the angel Gabriel to pelt the devil with stones. Abraham obeyed, using seven stones each time, until the devil disappeared. Thus, each of three pillars at Mina represented an appearance of the devil. This part of the *haj* would last for three days.

The stoning ritual was what Cindy had feared the most. So many people would be there, all throwing stones, trying to hit the pillars seven times each. If they missed they must try again and again, throwing until they succeeded. People were struck with stones, and sometimes crushed in the crowds moving from one pillar to another. Fortunately, they arrived at 3:00 a.m. for the first stoning, and the crowds were sparse at that hour.

As it was permissible to have someone else perform some rituals, it was decided that the men would perform the stoning ritual for the ladies on the second day. As their bus was making its way back to the hotel for the night, word suddenly spread that tragedy had struck at Mina. Several people at the stoning had been killed. Pulling their cell phones out, worried ladies were calling their husbands when Cindy noticed the youngest one on the bus, who was clearly desperate.

"My phone, it's no good! It has no charge!" she said to Cindy. "I am newlywed! I cannot reach my husband to know he is safe!" The poor young wife was hysterical.

"Here," Cindy said, handing over her phone. "Use my phone."

To everyone's great relief, none of the pilgrims who died were from the UAE, *alhamdallah.* The following year, the pillars were replaced with walls, making the stoning ritual easier, more organized, and safer.

In the final day of their *haj,* the third day of stoning, it poured rain. The soggy streets, encumbered as they were with construction equipment and mud, quickly flooded. Roads were blocked, detours nonexistent, and the bus driver, who was not a local, became hopelessly lost when the traffic finally began to move. He made turn after turn, only to come to a standstill in more traffic, unsure where he was headed. As the hours ticked by the trip, which was only supposed to take a couple of hours, was taking far longer. Some of the women on the bus were becoming angry with the driver. Cindy tried to calm them.

"God is testing your *haj,*" she said, quoting the Quran: "Seek help with patient perseverance and prayer, for God is with those who patiently persevere." Yet privately, she sorely wished she'd brought those apples instead of taking them out of her handbag and leaving them in the hotel room. There was no food on the bus, and some of the women were diabetic. Also, after so many hours, everyone's cell phone batteries were running out. The women were upset that they couldn't contact their husbands to let them know what was happening.

Thank God, I brought that extra battery. Cindy called the hotel and gave her phone to the driver so they could give him directions. When they finally arrived, their two-hour excursion had lasted fourteen hours. Cindy was stiff and sore, hungry, and her feet and ankles were swollen. But she was thankful they'd made it. As the bus pulled up at the hotel, some of the men who had been waiting rushed up, pulled the driver out, and threatened to beat him.

Mohammed and the other men intervened. "No, no, do not beat him! That's enough! Respect yourselves! Take it easy, our wives are safe now, thank God." Anger and violence were forbidden, especially on a religious journey.

With that, their *haj* officially ended. There were no more rituals to perform. They were free to relax, visit and pray in the mosque, shop for the gifts the children were expecting, and see the sights around Mecca.

The *haj* was a life-changing experience for Cindy. She had conquered her fears and become closer to God. She had even discovered that sometimes she, the American convert, could help others to be better Muslims. She'd made lifelong friends. She could proudly claim that she'd made her pilgrimage. She was a *Hajiya.*

The next month, March, the United States invaded Iraq.

"God punish them for what they do to the Iraqi people," Cindy heard as she entered Faisal's elementary school.

"Hush, there is an American here."

"Who? Where? Oh, her? No, that's Sindiya. Don't worry; she's one of us."

She's one of us. In that moment, Cindy knew it was true. She was American, she was still Cindy Lou Davis from Mocksville, North Carolina, but she was one of them now. Those remembered tears, the ones she had shed those first days, just wanting to be one of them, welled up in her eyes again but this time they were tears of gratitude. They accepted her as one of them. And she understood what they were saying about the attack on Iraq. It didn't make sense. Anyone could see that Saddam Hussein had nothing to do with the 911 attacks. But they were blaming the American government, not the American people. Not her.

President Saddam Hussein was a ruthless dictator who controlled his own and neighboring countries through military force and imprisonment, poisoning and murdering his adversaries. And yet, to Arabs across the Middle East, the U.S. invasion was an attempt to control the oil supply, and they also believed that America was intervening in the Middle East because of its support for Israel in the ongoing Arab-Israeli conflict. They could see nothing good coming of it for the Iraqi people. The U.S. attack would only destroy the fragile stability in the region. The result would be less democracy and less peace, and it would only open the door for terrorism to grow.

In the twenty years since she'd come to the Middle East as a young bride, barely out of her teens and oblivious to world events, living alongside the people in her adopted country had opened Cindy's eyes and forced her to see things not just as an American but from their point of view as well. Despite their nationalism and preference to marry within the family, the Emirati population was a mixture of people from all over the region. The Bedouins, the sheikhs, and others had taken wives from around the region over many centuries. Everyone had Saudi relatives, or relatives in Bahrain, Qatar, Oman, Iran, Iraq. There were people from Lebanon, Pakistan, India, Malaysia, Yemen, Syria, Jordan, and Kuwait, who had forged connections through marriage and the ever-widening web of family.

Some marriages were the result of war, poverty or desperation. A widow, sister, or a cousin was rescued, and a marriage was arranged that could save a woman's life. If she was divorced, or had committed some real or perceived crime, if she had caused her family dishonor, she could be punished or even killed in her home country, often by her own family, and the crime could go unanswered. In the poorest, strictest, most conservative families, honor and respectability were everything. Sometimes worth more than a life. Women who faced those dangers where they came from were safe in the UAE. The UAE was founded on the modern principles of tolerance and basic human rights.

Cindy had come to the UAE under different circumstances, for a different reason, but she understood the underlying values of honor and respectability. For her, they stood right alongside faith and love of God, and she was always careful to mind the customs and adhere to the cultural norms in her adopted country. It never occurred to her to question whether a woman should cover or wear the veil, or question why she didn't drive, or criticize her for depending on a nanny or housemaid. She never questioned someone who was a second or third wife. It was their culture. She may not always understand it, but who was she to criticize?

Likewise, she was not changed by any questions or criticism she heard. Marrying Mohammed and becoming a Muslim had not transformed her into someone she was not. Cindy knew that people talked; it was a national pastime in the UAE. She did things differently than the locals. She did things her way. She cleaned her own house, she cooked, she fixed things. If people didn't like it, so be it. She was proud of her Emirati-American family. People could take it or leave it.

Chapter 18: English Teacher

2006

Faisal was in fifth grade, and there was a problem with his teacher. It wasn't just that she was, in general, poorly suited to teaching, lacking the energy and personality to motivate students. Only after she'd been hired as an English teacher did it emerge that she didn't know English very well. She mispronounced words, misspelled them on the board, and made grammatical errors. Faisal, who had outgrown his childish resistance and now spoke and wrote perfect English, came home with stories about her inexcusable mistakes, which Cindy reluctantly passed on to the school administrators. She didn't want to get the woman in trouble or fired, but the students weren't learning. They were falling behind, and it wasn't fair. She couldn't stand by and do nothing.

Thinking that perhaps teaching fifth grade English was too difficult, the principal decided to put the teacher into the first grade. The results were disastrous. She stood before the first-graders just as she had in fifth, writing on the board, reciting to the children in broken, incorrect English, and expecting them to repeat and learn. She used no flash cards, no pictures, no games. The children responded by squirming, poking each other, and talking – in Arabic. The principal had to face it – the kids would never learn English unless something was done. With so much development happening in the country, and so many new subjects being taught, getting qualified teachers was harder than ever. They had to recruit from overseas countries like England and the United States. All the best ones went to Dubai and Abu Dhabi. A little town like Khorfakkan had to take the teachers that didn't get jobs elsewhere.

The principal had seen Cindy working with the parents at the meetings for several years, using Power Point to teach about health and education. Cindy spoke English and Arabic. Maybe she would help.

"Sindiya, could you help us, please?" the principal asked. "Would you be willing to come in three days a week and teach the art and music enrichment classes in English? We can't pay you very much. But we really need to do something."

"Well, I don't know. I suppose I can try."

"Just start at the beginning. Colors. The alphabet. Anything, just teach them something!"

Cindy had demurred out of modestly, but the truth was that she relished this opportunity. It was what she'd been waiting for, training for without even realizing it. She had been using Power Point for years, ever since 1998. She'd been playing with it, adding animation, sounds, and all the new bells and whistles whenever she got the updates. Google was her best friend. Power Point was her love. She'd been staying up at night creating projects just for the fun of it. Now, she had a chance to put her creativity, curiosity, and self-taught computer savvy to work.

Using the textbooks as a guide, Cindy made units following the first-grade curriculum. Each lesson had an interactive Power Point to go with it. A giant ice cream cone taught colors. A numbers train put the numbers in order with the words in Arabic first and then – *WHOOSH!* – the English word swooped in to replace it. A funny face told them when an answer was wrong, a happy face when it was correct. The children were tickled, and they learned quickly. Some of the kids in the class were the children of teachers at the school. "At least we hear English words out of our kids now," they said. "Before, it was like they weren't even speaking English." It was true. Cindy had added her voice when she heard the kids mispronouncing common words. "Who told you it was lie-*oon*? It's *lie-on*!"

At the end of the school year, Cindy copied the lessons onto CDs and distributed them to the first graders in the school. Soon, teachers were requesting copies. "How much will you sell it for? We'll pay you for it." Her cost for each CD was one dirham. Thinking that it would only be a few teachers at her school, Cindy decided to sell them for ten dirhams – about $2.50 U.S.

They caught on like wildfire. With the first-grade CDs making the rounds, parents and teachers were clamoring for more. "We need you to do the second grade. And third grade." By the end of June, with the textbooks as her guide and Google as her resource, Cindy had built lessons for the second and third grades, distributing the CDs to the teachers, who sold them to the students. Over the summer, she made CDs for the fourth and fifth grades. By the end of that first year, she had netted 5,000 dirhams – $1300 U.S.

It was only the beginning. Now people were asking for sixth grade.

"I don't have time to do the sixth grade," she protested. They didn't understand how complex the upper grades were. Fifth grade had taken so much time that she was charging 25 dirhams for it, and some people were asking why. They didn't know how much time she'd put into it. Others didn't care – they were glad to pay any price. Their children were learning English, albeit with a southern accent.

That year during the Heritage Celebration, the Higher Colleges of Technology had a booth. Yasmeen urged Cindy to go over to meet the American official sitting at the table. Cindy resisted, her modesty preventing her from marching up and introducing herself.

"He speaks English," Yasmeen said. "You have to meet him." Dragging Cindy over, she introduced them. Once the conversation got going, Cindy relaxed and chatted with the man. After a few minutes, he looked at her quizzically.

"Cindy," he said, "where are you *from?*" Seeing herself through his eyes, Cindy had to laugh. Here she was, dressed as a typical Emirati woman speaking perfect English with a regional lilt that he recognized.

"I'm from North Carolina."

"What town?"

"Mocksville."

"Why, I'm from Charlotte!" the man exclaimed.

"That's where I met my husband." What a small world. From that moment on, Bill Lex and his wife Diane became good friends with Cindy. It was a friendship that would last long after the American couple had moved back to the United States.

Cindy made sure through her connection with Bill that the Sharjah Ministry of Education was aware of her CD's. The lessons made their way out of Khorfakkan schools, spreading out to the schools in the Emirate of Sharjah. As word of her work spread, Cindy was invited to make presentations at meetings throughout the district. The name Cindy Davis became well-known at the Sharjah Ministry of Education and at schools all around the emirate.

"Buy these CDs and use them in your class," supervisors all over Sharjah were telling their teachers. Cindy could hardly believe that her programs were so popular. She'd gotten everything from the Internet, and they could do the same, so easily. The lessons were all out there, the worksheets were there – she hadn't invented any of it, just taken what was available for and put it together. But these teachers hadn't caught up with the technology. Cindy had no teaching training or experience. But here she was, developing and teaching lessons, and teaching teachers how to teach. She made sure that her CDs were write-protected so that nobody could claim to a supervisor that her work was theirs.

There were kids all over the Emirate of Sharjah, speaking English with her North Carolina accent. How had this happened? It had all started with Mohammed, when he brought home that first computer and said, "Here, Honey. I bought you this computer. You are smart. You will figure out what to do with it."

The children grew up, as children do. Cindy no longer had kids in the schools but the teachers still begged her, "Come and be on our Mothers' Council."

"But I don't have any kids here."

"Never mind, no problem! We'll be your kids."

Those years working in the schools were the best years of her life, but she had to move on. She would have loved to get a job in the Ministry of Education, but it required a degree or a certain level of experience, which she did not have. Despite everything she'd accomplished, and everything she was known for, on paper it looked like Cindy didn't know anything. She had a business school certificate, and that was it. No diploma, no job history or experience – nothing. They couldn't hire her.

Aminah was a student in the Bachelor of Education program at Fujairah Women's College, one of the Higher Colleges of Technology – HCT.

Cindy knew Aminah's teachers, and had been working with the girls in the education program, going around to schools with them and doing presentations on the importance of speaking English, just as she had when she was on the Mothers' Council.

HCT attracted students from all along the East Coast, and had programs in Applied Communications, Business, Computer Information Science, Education, Engineering Technology & Science, and Health Sciences. It also had a first-year Foundations program in which all courses were taught in English, to ease the students into college life and prepare them for when they started the more rigorous programs.

Cindy was hired for a one-semester temporary position, working in the admissions office. If she were to keep it, she knew she needed to prove herself. Part of her job was working with the incoming Foundations students, and she realized quickly that the girls coming into HCT were different than American students starting college. Having been protected by their culture and socially isolated among others just like themselves, their level of maturity was more at middle school than high school, let alone college. And their English was weak. She told the Foundations teachers about the Power Points she'd made for the elementary schools, and suggested that she could do the same for the HCT Foundations course. Using the Foundations book, she created Units One through Fourteen. At her supervisor's suggestion, she recruited speakers of several different nationalities to help record the audio. That way, they would be exposed to and understand various accents.

The Foundations lessons were a success. Cindy soon found herself making Power Point presentations for teachers and administrators for every meeting or event that was on the calendar. And she was the go-to person for computer troubleshooting. Never mind that they had a tech specialist and a computer science department. Everybody came to Cindy first. When Cindy's contract ended, she was rehired for another semester. And another. The second year, Aisha started at HCT, in the Applied Communications program.

Working at HCT was another dream job for Cindy, but she didn't like her temporary status. The pay was less, and she didn't get benefits. If she wanted to be hired on a three-year contract, which as an expat with an American passport included a round-trip ticket home each year, she needed a degree. It was the same problem she'd run into at the Ministry of Education.

At HCT, Cindy was working alongside expats every day. Most of the people she worked with were from America or the UK. Her direct supervisor, Sule, was Turkish. They became great friends. One day Sule gave Cindy the greatest compliment ever.

"You know, Cindy," Sule said. "All these people around here, they actually have degrees. Masters degrees, doctorates. You don't have a degree, but you can still do everything. It just shows how sometimes it's not necessarily the people with the most impressive degrees that are the most valuable ones." There was a program she could enroll in to get a degree that would fulfill the requirements to be hired, but it would take two years and cost 8,000 dirhams, or about $2000 U.S. Was it worth it?

"Honey," Mohammed said, "you are smart. You should do it. Don't worry about the money. We can pay for it. You need to get the degree so that you can get the benefits." He always supported her in anything she wanted to do. She took the classes, got the degree, and signed the three-year contract.

Chapter 19: 30 Years

2012

In the three decades since Cindy met Mohammed, the UAE had grown into the modern, globalized country that Sheikh Zayed envisioned. Emiratis were exposed to the outside world through television and the Internet. Dubai was known around the globe as a world-class city with glittering glass towers and the world's first indoor ski resort. The Burj Khalifa was the world's tallest building, and the Dubai Mall was the world's largest mall. No longer were movies, clothing, and handbags from America or Europe hard to get. The malls were filled with them. Cindy could go to Dubai and eat at her favorite American restaurants – TGI Friday's, Texas Roadhouse, The Olive Garden, The Hard Rock Café. The latest movies were playing at multi-plex theaters in the malls.

In Khorfakkan, people were still conservative, some becoming stricter about religion, gender roles, and traditional ways, perhaps as a reaction to what they saw as a takeover by Western culture. There were still many women who didn't drive, who lived behind the veil and didn't speak with any man who wasn't part of the family. They were protected, and had either no desire or no opportunity to be out in the world. Workers and shop keepers were foreign men, and husbands handled the business. Sometimes fathers or brothers objected to young women getting their driver's licenses. One day Cindy and Mohammed sent word to Zamzam and the stepsons that Aminah would be getting her driver's license. The next thing they knew, the two younger sons were in the house, making a scene.

"No! It's impossible!" they said. "Wait until she is married. Then it is the husband's problem." Their alarm seemed unreasonable, but Mohammed wanted to keep the peace.

"Let it go," he said to Cindy. "It doesn't matter. Please, drop it. For my sanity."

Cindy shook her head. "Look," she said, "I can't be here all the time to drive them everywhere. If you don't want her to drive," she said to her stepsons, "then you get her a driver."

"OK, all right! Fine. We will get a driver." They would get her a driver, or they would have to be the drivers.

Cindy didn't understand how these men, who she had helped to raise, had become so conservative. But as always, she did not push it. She had learned, over the years, that this was how things were. It was never just your decision; there were always other people involved. To Aminah, she said, "Just be patient. You will get your reward down the road. God doesn't forget the sacrifices you make."

Gladys was getting older, and she'd never been to the UAE. Nobody in the family had. It was almost thirty years, and Cindy had made a dozen trips back home to see them, but none of them had ever seen her adopted home. Every time Cindy had asked her mother to come, there was a reason not to. First, she was waiting until there were grandchildren to visit. Then Mohammed was sent back for the three years of training. Then R.G. had died. Now Gladys was church treasurer, and you'd think that the Gospel Church couldn't survive for a couple of weeks without Gladys Davis minding the books. And there was a dispute involving her grandmother's property near the university in Chapel Hill, and Gladys didn't want to leave until it was settled. Finally, Cindy decided to enlist her Aunt Peggy's help to force her mother's hand. She was afraid that soon it would be too late. She had her own money now that she was working full-time, and didn't have to ask Mohammed for it – not that he wouldn't give it in a heartbeat if she asked.

"Here's the deal," she told Aunt Peggy. "I will pay for everything – your ticket, Mom's ticket – you just bring a little bit of pocket money. I'll plan everything."

"You're making it very difficult for me to say no …" Aunt Peggy said.

"That is what I want to do!" Cindy said. "Tell me how I can make it even more difficult, because I don't want you to say no. I want you to agree to come visit me now, or after Christmas – whatever – and I know if I can get you on board, you can convince Mom. Just get her here. Do whatever it takes." Cindy knew that Gladys would listen to her sister.

Peggy was the younger one, but she was the organizer, and Gladys would do whatever Peggy told her to do. Cindy happily started to plan everything, down to the last detail.

They came after the Christmas holidays. In thirty years of travel, Cindy had never once missed a connecting flight. To her dismay, the weather was bad and Gladys and Peggy missed both of their connections – Charlotte to Atlanta, and then Atlanta to Dubai. When they finally arrived, they had a belated Christmas with gifts in Khorfakkan before heading to Dubai for a few days of sightseeing.

They checked in at the Atlantis hotel on The Palm Jumeirah – the first of three palm-shaped artificial islands in the shape of palms jutting out into the sea off the coast of Dubai. When Cindy arrived in 1982, the land and coastline surrounding Dubai were plain and barren. Since then the skyscrapers had risen higher and higher, and starting with the first reclamation project in 2001, the shoreline had been transformed. In a feat that grabbed the attention of engineers, civic leaders, and environmentalists around the world, developers piled sand dredged from the bottom of the sea to build the fanciful islands that would attract tourists from around the world. The first was a small island with a luxury high-rise, hotel named Al Arab. Its shape, resembling a sail, had made it a world-famous landmark and symbol of Dubai. When Cindy checked into the ultra-luxurious Atlantis – The Palm with Gladys and Aunt Peggy, it had been open for just over four years.

The first item on their itinerary was a trip to Dubai Mall. At the main entrance, they watched Ferraris, Porsches, and Lamborghinis worth millions of dollars pull up at the valet car park. In the basement of the mall, they found the entrance to At the Top – the observation deck on the 124th floor of the Burj Khalifa. A long escalator ride brought them to a high-speed elevator that took them up, ears popping. They walked around inside the building and outside on the observation deck, taking in the panoramic views of the booming city and its forest of building cranes. It was like being in an airplane that was flying over the city to land. Back on the ground, they visited the Dubai Aquarium and Underwater Zoo inside the mall – the Atlantic, where they were staying, also had an aquarium, but Cindy thought the one at Dubai Mall was better.

The next day, because traffic had become so congested in Dubai, roads were always under construction, and parking was difficult and expensive, Cindy had booked a Wonderbus tour. The land and sea vehicle took them to Dubai Creek – the same area that Cindy had gazed down upon as she landed in Dubai as a bride in 1982. They toured the historical district with its narrow streets, museums, old *souk,* and *abra* station. Their bus took them across the water to the *Deira,* where they browsed the spice shops and sampled sweets. They watched as cargo was unloaded from the old-fashioned wooden *dhows* lining the waterfront and piled onto carts and small pickup trucks, which disappeared into the teeming streets and narrow passageways of the *Deira.* This part of the city hadn't changed as much in the past two decades – once the first skyscrapers were built, development had moved inland to the new Financial District, and further south along the shore to a new Marina District.

The next day they made the one-hour drive south from Dubai to Abu Dhabi. Their first stop was the magnificent Sheikh Zayed Grand Mosque. As they drove across the two-year-old Sheikh Zayed Bridge, they saw the shimmering white mosque, four great minarets surrounding dozens of domes of different sizes, rising to their left. Construction had begun in 1996 by Sheikh Zayed, who had envisioned it as a place to showcase the blending of traditional Islamic culture with modern architecture. Zayed died in 2004 and the mosque, including his tomb, was completed in 2007.

All women entering the Grand Mosque, including non-Muslims, were required to cover. The mosque provided *abayas* and *shaylas* for visitors, but Cindy had brought two from her collection for Gladys and Peggy – she and the girls had closets full, all sizes, at home – so they didn't have to wait in line. They entered the giant courtyard, walking on the cool Italian marble inlaid with flowers, where they removed their shoes before entering the main Prayer Hall with a tour group.

"This is the world's largest Persian carpet," the guide said in perfect English, going on to explain the construction history of the mosque and the prayer schedule.

This place has changed so much since I first came here, Cindy thought. She barely recognized it, but she knew that the old Army base where Mohammed worked when they were first married had been close to where the Grand Mosque now stood. The 1960's-era Maqtaa Bridge, which until recently everyone crossed to get onto Abu Dhabi island, still stood, but was overshadowed by the great and imposing new Zayed Bridge.

Their afternoon destination was the Emirates Palace Hotel. Like the Grand Mosque, it was built by the government as a showcase for Arab culture. Walking through the entrance onto the marble floor of the main lobby, Cindy pointed up at the spectacular dome ceiling.

"That's real gold," she told Gladys and Peggy. "Everywhere that you see gold in here, it's the real thing. They even have an ATM that gives out gold. It was the first of its kind."

Cindy had booked a reservation for three for high tea. They settled into plush chairs in the busy café, where they could watch the bustling business of the hotel from a raised platform, and enjoyed scones, finger sandwiches dusted with gold, and mini tartlets decorated with gold-tipped leaves.

Aunt Peggy had noticed that many people spoke English. "You wouldn't really need to speak Arabic here, would you?" she observed.

"Not now, you wouldn't," Cindy agreed. Things had changed so much. Billboards and signs were all in both English and Arabic. All the expat workers spoke English – people working in the malls, hotels, and attractions. All the men of Mohammed's generation knew English. And the young people of Aminah's, Aisha's, and Faisal's age, they knew English. The ones who were left out, who were caught in between, were the women of Cindy's generation. They were the ones who had never learned English.

As exciting as it was to be in Dubai and Abu Dhabi, Gladys and Peggy's favorite thing was to sit in Cindy's courtyard with their shoes off, baking their bare toes in the sun and watching the bananas growing in the banana tree. Her normally lively mother seemed to have less energy than Cindy remembered. She chalked it up to jet lag, and Gladys getting older. Cindy had put in a bench and a swing, anything to accommodate them and make them feel welcome and comfortable. They loved the balmy weather. They loved the rugged mountains. They loved Cindy's house – to them, it was huge. And they loved that banana tree.

Gladys and Aunt Peggy had always thrown a party for Cindy before she left, and at the end of the two weeks Cindy threw a party for them. She set up tables outside in the car park beside the house, and hired a caterer to cook a variety of American and Emirati dishes and set them up in a buffet. She ordered a cake. Aisha and Aminah made decorations and party favors. Cindy invited expat friends from work and the less conservative friends and neighbors. Jameela and her young daughters were there. Mohammed's family – Zamzam and Mohammed's sons, his daughter Maryam and her family, and the aunties, uncles, and cousins, including the beloved Auntie Fatima – all stayed away because it was a "mixed party." Before dinner, the men sat in Mohammed's *majlis* and the ladies in Cindy's living room. The men were called to the buffet first, and ladies were called separately. They ate at separate tables, but in the same space, where they could see each other. That was too modern for Mohammed's relatives.

That summer, Cindy and Mohammed celebrated their 30th anniversary with another party. She had loved the party she threw for her mother and aunt so much that she used the same caterer, the same decorations. She invited her expat friends from the college and Mohammed, who had retired from the military and was working for a consulting company on the base, invited some expats from work. The men and women were served and seated separately, but as soon as the first round of plates were emptied, people began to shift. Women rose to join their husbands at their tables, meeting their colleagues. Jameela and her daughters occupied a corner table with a view of the room, smiling, talking, and posing for photos. Cindy and Mohammed opened their anniversary gifts. Mohammed's gift to Cindy was a jewelry set with gold and diamond necklace, bracelets, and earrings.

Over the past three decades Cindy had assimilated, but she hadn't changed. She was a faithful Muslim and could speak perfect Arabic, sounding just like a local. She wore the *abaya* and *shayla*. To her, they were a symbol of her Muslim faith, and her commitment to Mohammed. She had put up with a lot over the years – living with his family, waiting to get her own place. Doing without. Sure, Mohammed did things that got on her nerves sometimes – like the mess he always made in the bathroom with that water hose before he went to pray. But if that was the worst thing he did, she was lucky. She had made sacrifices, but in the long run, she had gained. She had everything she'd ever wanted, and more. She had a job she likes, her own money, and could buy whatever she wanted. She'd had a housemaid for a few years now, so she didn't have to worry about housework, laundry, or cooking. Cindy and Neela, the maid from Sri Lanka, had become good friends. They were the same age and, when Neela had some spare time, they talked about their lives and families in their home countries.

Zamzam had tried to interfere, but she had never been able to come between them. In recent years, she had mellowed. No longer did they have to speak in code around her, no longer did Cindy and her daughters have to hide their *abayas* lest Zamzam see them and think they were going out without her.

The week after the anniversary party, Zamzam was having dental work done, and Jassim would take her. Cindy, knowing that her mother-in-law would be terrified, offered to go along. As Zamzam's tiny frame, cloaked in black, was led down the hallway toward the surgery room, she turned.

"I want Umm Faisal – I want Umm Faisal with me!" Zamzam cried. Hearing her name, Cindy caught her breath, her heart expanding inside her chest. Zamzam had been her biggest challenge. The woman was named after the holy well of Mecca, the water from God that the angel had drawn from the desert to rescue Ibrahim's wife Hajar and her baby. Zamzam had forced Cindy to take a stand, over and over. Despite herself Zamzam had taught her, through challenge after challenge, to become ever more steadfast in her unity with her husband. She had forced Mohammed, over and over, to come to Cindy's defense, to reassure her that God was watching and that rewards awaited her.

It was Zamzam who had put out that first bowl to catch the rainwater, God's water from Heaven, when Cindy was a newlywed bride learning the customs in her new country. Afterward, whenever she could, Cindy had always set out a container to gather water from Heaven. She welcomed clouds, she watched for them. Whenever there were clouds, there was a chance to catch some water from Heaven. Now, another reward.

"Umm Faisal!" Zamzam called. "Umm Faisal!"

"Yes, Umm Mohammed," Cindy answered, moving toward her mother-in-law. "I'm coming. I will stay with you."

Cindy opens anniversary gifts in the family majlis/living room

Mohammed and Cindy open anniversary gifts in the formal majlis

Cindy and Mohammed open a 30th anniversary gift, June 21, 2012

Epilogue

In the summer of 2012, Cindy flew home to Mocksville. Gladys wasn't feeling well, and while Cindy was there, they received the diagnosis. Gladys had breast cancer. She died on August 2, 2012, with Cindy by her side. Cindy was glad that her mother had finally had a chance to see with her own eyes that Cindy had a good and happy life in the UAE. She brought back a few small mementos, little gifts and curios that reminded her of her mother, and set them in a special cabinet in her home as a memorial to her mother.

That winter, Cindy's niece Emily, Randy's daughter, came to visit during her Christmas break. Aisha and Aminah welcomed their cousin with open arms, and they took Emily on a whirlwind tour of Dubai and Abu Dhabi. Despite the many years of not seeing each other, the cousins were as close as ever.

Cindy retired from HCT in the fall of 2014, and was looking forward to a December visit from Randy, his wife Cindy and their stepdaughter. She received a phone call in September. Randy had been diagnosed with colon cancer. He entered treatment, and the trip went on as planned, albeit with Randy in a wheelchair. They went to the Burj Khalifa and viewed the spectacular New Year's Eve fireworks from their hotel room across town. They went to Global Village, a huge exposition with shopping pavilions from countries all over the world, several stages with live cultural performances, and an amusement park with a giant Ferris wheel. Cindy booked a Desert Safari trip complete with dune bashing, camel rides, dinner, and belly dancing. It was the experience of a lifetime for them all.

Randy passed away on June 16, 2016. Cindy, along with family and friends, was by his side. Randy had been a volunteer firefighter and a guest preacher at Woodleaf Baptist Church, filling in for the pastor, preaching God's love. During his funeral, firefighters and policemen lined up on the street and on every overpass, saluting as Randy's casket passed by, accompanied by dozens of fire trucks, ambulances, and police cars, lights flashing.

Her mother and closest brother were both gone, and with them went Cindy's strongest connections to Mocksville. It would always be home, but her thoughts turned toward her adopted country, the UAE. What if something happened to Mohammed and she, as a U.S. citizen, had to leave? Without an Emirati passport, there was no guarantee that she could stay. Khorfakkan was her home, her children were there, and they would remain there. She decided to apply for her Emirati passport, to become an Emirati national.

Aminah got an administrative job working at HCT. Aisha produced two short documentary films while she was a student, both of which were accepted and screened at the Abu Dhabi Film Festival. The second film, "Enough is Enough," addressed the negative attitudes toward Emirati children with a foreign parent – "half-Emiratis." "Enough is Enough" received attention, was screened at the Dubai Film Festival as well as others. Aisha was featured in several newspapers and magazines, making her locally famous. She is currently finishing a Master's Degree program at Birmingham City University, which includes a teaching requirement which she fulfills teaching video production at HCT. Cindy accompanies Aisha as a companion on her frequent trips out of town to film festivals and events. They traveled to London in March 2017, and to the 2017 Cannes Film Festival in May, where Aisha volunteered as part of her degree program.

Because Aminah and Aisha are both working and have different schedules their brothers, who never got around to getting a driver, wearied of the responsibility of driving them. Both Aminah and Aisha now have their driver's licenses. They frequently attend weddings of friends and relatives with Cindy but, so far, they have had no offers of marriage.

Faisal earned a degree in engineering and is working for an oil company in Fujairah. Zamzam is pushing Cindy to find a wife for Faisal so that she can see her great-grandchildren. Cindy is in no hurry to find him a wife.

To Cindy's great sadness, Auntie Fatima passed away in 2016. Nobody knows exactly how old she was.

Mohammed is still working at Zayed Military City during the week, and he has told Cindy that he enjoys it and will keep on working "until they make me go away." When that happens, *inshallah,* it will be the first time they have lived together full-time since they were in the United States in the 1980's, except for the one year after he retired from the military and before he was hired by his current company.

As of this writing, Cindy's Emirati passport is still pending.

Khorfakkan Beach with hotel, 1989

Cindy and Mohammed's neighborhood

Khorfakkan Cinema

Doors in old neighborhood and new neighborhood

Large new homes under construction in Khorfakkan

Corniche road in Khorfakkan

Corniche shops and Shumayliyah Mountains, Khorfakkan, 2014

Beach at Khorfakkan Bay, with Holiday Inn (now Oceanic) hotel, 2014

Main Street Khorfakkan, 2012

Aminah and Cindy stroll Khorfakkan beach with an American friend, 2014

Acknowledgements

First, I want to thank Cindy Lou Davis for her patience and cooperation in the making of this book. I know there were times when she doubted that it was ever going to happen. She shared her story with me, and I am honored that she placed her faith and trust in me to tell it. Thanks also go to Aminah Al Hammadi and Aisha Al Hammadi for sharing their stories with me, and thanks to Mohammed, for his humor and his hospitality.

Thank you to the many friends I made living in Abu Dhabi through the American Women's Network, who encouraged me to write this book. Also, thanks to the readers of my blog, Wildcardtravels.blogspot.com, whose feedback on my writing and storytelling gave me the confidence to pursue the writing a book.

Thank you to the people who read drafts and gave feedback – Penny Schreiber, for her excellent editorial advice, and Karin Knowles, Michele Appel, Nicole Sterley, and Shana Bagley Howe for their insightful comments. Thank you to Pamela Thompson and the students at Khalifa City Women's College in Abu Dhabi who listened to an early draft of the first chapters and wanted more. After that I had to keep going. Thank you to Debra Loson, who listened to me read those early chapters as we sat by the pool in Abu Dhabi and said, "I want to know what happens next," even though she already knew. Again, her enthusiasm spurred me on. Thank you to Debra Loson and Donnette Cline Schofield for taking time to travel to Khorfakkan with me. And thank you, Lucy Osaer, for being the greatest cheerleader anyone could wish for.

Finally, thank you to my husband Mark, who shared with me his insights into the lifestyle and mindset of Emirati men. You always believed in me and encouraged this project with the love, space, and support I needed, and you prodded me to "just finish it" when it was clearly time. You are my hero.

Glossary

This is a selected list of words and expressions to help readers with pronunciation and familiarity. As spellings and pronunciations of words vary, I am using the spelling that I am most familiar with. I have provided phonetic pronunciation hints but, because different Arabic speakers have distinct speech patterns, they may not correspond exactly to the pronunciation in other regions.

abaya (ah-BUY-ah) – The traditional black cloak worn by Muslim women, now part of the Emirati National Dress for ladies. The once loose-fitting wrap has been modernized, and many women wear custom tailored and fitted designs incorporating decorative panels, sequins, and other embellishments.

abra (AH-brah) – A traditional small open wooden boat used for ferrying people across Dubai Creek. The cost is one dirham, or about 26 cents U.S., paid to the boat driver. The *abra* is an important form of transportation for workers as well as a draw for tourists looking to experience local color.

adhan (ahd-HAN) – The Islamic call to prayer, sung five times a day and broadcast from the minarets of mosques.

agal (ah-GAL) – The black rope worn around the head to hold the *ghutrah* in place. It is part of the Emirati National Dress for men.

ahlan wa sahlan (AH-lan-wa-sah-LAN) – A universal "welcome" greeting. Translated, *ahlan* means "family" and *sahlan* means "a place where abundant food is shared." Thus, the expression arose from the tradition of welcoming strangers into the family and showing hospitality.

Aisha (AH-sha) – A girl's name meaning "alive" in Arabic. It is a common name among Sunni Muslims.

alhamdullilah (al-HAM-du-LIL-ah) – An expression meaning "praise God," commonly used to express happiness or satisfaction.

al-salaam aalykum (al-sa-LAM-ah-LIKE-um) – The universal Arabic "hello" or "good morning/afternoon/evening" greeting, literally meaning "peace be upon you."

Aminah (AH-min-ah) – A girl's name meaning "trustworthy" in Arabic.

barasti hut (bah-RAH-stee) – Hut made of mud and palm branches

bismallah (bis-MAH-lah) – An expression used when beginning an activity, meaning "in the name of God."

corniche (corn-EESH) – A French word for a road along cliff or mountainside, used in the Middle East to name a waterfront promenade.

Deira (dee-ERR-a) – The historic commercial district of Dubai, along Dubai Creek

dhow – (dow) – A traditional wooden boat. There are several kinds, with sails or motors, but the ones on Dubai Creek have engines.

djin/djinni (jin/jinni) – Spirit beings that can be good or evil. In English, "genie" or "genies."

Faisal (FAY-sall) – A boy's name meaning "stubborn."

firni (FERN-ee) – A pudding made with milk and rice, served on special occasions. Originates from Afghanistan and Pakistan.

Fujairah (foo-JARE-ah) – A port city on the east coast of the United Arab Emirates, south of Khorfakkan, on the Indian Ocean.

ghutrah (GOO-trah) – headdress worn by Emirati men as part of the National Dress, a white piece of cloth held in place by the black rope called *agal*.

haj (haj) – The holy pilgrimage to Mecca that each Muslim is expected to make at least once in his or her lifetime.

halal (hah-LAL) – Something that is permitted per Islamic (Sharia) law, including food, drink, and daily activities.

halwa (HAL-wah) – A sweet dessert with a fudge-like consistency made with either flour and butter or nut butter.

haram (hah-RAHM) – An activity that is forbidden or considered sinful by Islamic law.

harees (hah-REES) – A porridge-like Middle Eastern dish made with cracked wheat mixed with meat.

hijab (hee-job) – A head covering or scarf worn by Muslim women.

iftar – (IF-tar) – The evening meal that breaks the fast during Ramadan.

Ihram (IH-rahm) – Clothing worn during the haj signifying that all people are equal before God. Men wear two white sheets wrapped around the body and women typically wear white dresses.

imam (e-MOM) – An Islamic leader, most often the person who leads the prayers in a mosque.

inshallah (in-SHAHL-lah) – Literally, "if it is God's will," this expression is employed universally dozens of times each day whenever the future tense is used.

Jameela (Jah-MEEL-ah) – A girl's name meaning beautiful, graceful, and elegant.

Kaaba (ka-AH-bah) – The square building at the center of Islam's most sacred mosque, the Masjid-al-Haram, in Mecca.

kandura (kan-DER-ah) – The loose-fitting white robe worn by Arab men, part of the National Dress in the UAE. Also called thobe or dishdasha, among other names in other countries. Men in the UAE are renowned for their perfectly starched, spotless kaduras which they change several times a day.

khor – (kor) – Creek.

Khorfakkan (kor-fah-KHAN) – A small port town on the east coast of the UAE north of Fujairah where Mohammed was born, where he and Cindy raised their family, and where they all still live.

majlis (MAHJ-lis) – a large room where Arabs receive guests and hold meetings and discussions. Equivalent to a Western formal living room.

mashallah (MAH-shallah) – literally, "as God will it" to express thanks and appreciation for something or someone.

muzzein (moo-EH-zin) – The person who performs the *adhan,* or call to prayer, chosen for his good character and voice, who is relied upon to maintain the prayer schedule.

rakat (rah-kaht) – The ritualized Muslim prayer, including words and movements.

Ramadan (RAH-mah-don) – The month of fasting and prayer that occurs during the ninth month of the Islamic calendar in which Muslims fast from sunup until sundown.

sabkha (SAHB-kah) – A salt flat just above the high tide zone.

salat-al-janaza (salat-al- jah-NAH-zah) – The Muslim funeral prayer asking for God's mercy on the deceased and all who are deceased.

samboosa (sam-BOO-sah) – An Emirati pastry triangle filled with a meat and onion mixture and deep-fried.

shaytan (shay-tan) – A mischievous or evil *djinn.* Their leader is *Shaytan* (Satan.)

shukran (SHOO-kran) – Thank you.

suhoor (SOO-hoor) – The pre-dawn meal during Ramadan that must last until after sundown.

tawaf (TAH-wuf) – The ritual of circling the Kaaba during haj.

wa aalykuma asalaam (wa-ah-LEYE-kuma-ahsa-LAM) – A reciprocal greeting to *al-salaam alykum,* literally meaning "and peace be with you." It is comparable to responding to "hello" in English with "hello."

wadi (WAH-di) – A dry riverbed or ravine that flash floods during rains.

wasta (WAY-stah) – Influence gained from family connections or important acquaintances.

yalla (YA-lah) – Let's go.

Questions for Reading Groups

1. Why did Cindy and Felicia make the rule not to talk to the "Arab guys," and then not only break it but agree to date them?

2. Cindy was so determined that her fate was to be with Mohammed that she refused to consider any other possibility. What would you have done under those circumstances? What questions would be going through your mind?

3. Did Cindy's parents believe that the wedding would happen? What kinds of conversations do you think they had when they realized that their daughter was going to marry Mohammed?

4. How would you prepare yourself to make such a huge change in your life? How was Cindy prepared, and how was she not prepared, for her new life?

5. How would you have dealt with Zamzam?

6. What factors influenced Cindy's decision to convert to Islam? Do you think she should have waited? Why did Mohammed caution her not to rush?

7. How did the three years in the United States affect Cindy and Mohammed?

8. During Desert Storm, Cindy's family wanted her to come home. What do you think were their fears, and were they justified?

9. Cindy decided not to move to Abu Dhabi. If she had, how do you think it would have worked out?

10. Cindy witnessed supernatural phenomena. Have you? Do you believe in supernatural beings?

11. How did going to Arabic classes enhance Cindy's life and provide opportunities later?

12. Compare Cindy as a mother in the UAE to the kind of mother she would have been in the USA.

13. How does Cindy's response to 911 compare to yours?

14. Cindy finally got her own house in 2002 after twenty years of marriage. What does this say about her, and her relationship with Mohammed?

15. Was Cindy's haj successful? Why?

16. How did technology give Cindy the opportunity to make a difference in her community? What did it do for her quality of life?

17. What does the 30th anniversary party symbolize?

18. How was Cindy's relationship with Zamzam resolved?

19. If Cindy hadn't married Mohammed, what kind of education might she have gotten, and what kind of career might she have had? Would she have married a local boy?

20. What did marriage to Mohammed offer Cindy that she would have not gotten otherwise?

21. Is Cindy a different person at the end of the book than she was at the beginning? In what ways is she the same, and in what ways different?

22. What assumptions about the lives of Muslims, especially women, did you have before reading this book? Do you still hold those opinions?

23. How is the UAE like a Western country, and how is it different?

About the Author

Anne Schreiber Thomas grew up in St. Clair Shores, Michigan, a suburb of Detroit. She holds a B.A. in Geography (Earth Sciences) from Sonoma State University, and an M.S. in Geography from the University of Nevada, Reno. Ms. Thomas has lived in several San Francisco Bay Area cities, as well as Abu Dhabi. She has been a teacher, a conservation project manager, and a sailmaker, among other things. She lives with her husband in Gardnerville, Nevada when she isn't traveling or sailing. Find her author page on Facebook @wildcardtravels and read her blog, including stories about sailing as well as her adventures as an expat, at Wildcardtravels.blogspot.com.

About the Cover Artist

Maria Baj was born and raised in Lahore, Pakistan. She has been living in Abu Dhabi for more than two decades and has witnessed the economic and social evolution of the UAE. She started her art career as a silk painter with a focus on Arabic landscapes and lifestyle, and developed her unique style in acrylic and mixed media painting with rich colors and complex layers of texture while working at Art Central Abu Dhabi as an art instructor. Contact her at Mariabaj.com.

Made in the USA
Lexington, KY
10 June 2017